41 WAYS TO BUILD A BETTER YOUTH GROUP

BY MIKE BOGARD

F&L
FAITH & LIFE
PRESS

Newton, Kansas
Winnipeg, Manitoba

Printed in the United States of America.

International Standard Book Number 0-87303-226-8
Library of Congress Number 95-61921

Editorial direction by Susan E. Janzen; editing by Eddy Hall; copyediting by
Mary L. Gaeddert; design by Jim L. Friesen; printing by Mennonite Press, Inc.
Cover art by Ron Wheeler.

CONTENTS

PART 4: MISSION

RESOURCES FOR A YOUTH LEADER'S FIRST TOOLBOX

HELP, I'M A YOUTH LEADER!

"I'm a youth leader, now what?" If you are asking this question, you deserve answers and this book brings them to you.

You deserve answers because you have said yes to the challenge and privilege of leading your youth group.

You deserve answers because you have joined a quiet revolution that is changing the lives of North American youth.

You deserve answers because you are a caring Christian adult creatively and compassionately inviting youth to Christian faith and discipling them to follow Jesus Christ.

Like many youth leaders, you wonder...

- How can we generate excitement for youth ministry in our church?
- How can we train youth to lead?
- How can we teach the ancient biblical story to Generation Y?
- How can we work with youth to be the church together and with others?
- How can we inspire youth to live and share their faith in their self-oriented world?
- How can we build a better youth group?

Your youth group is one of thousands, large and small, that quietly gathers on Sunday evening or midweek all over North America. They meet in church basements and homes. They are led by youth and adults. They study the Bible and play games. They worship together and serve others. They meet to discover what it means to follow Jesus Christ and be the church. For these youth, yours included, the youth group can be their most meaningful experience of church.

That is why you and other youth group leaders are constantly searching for ways to build a better youth group. Whether you are a new or experienced youth group leader, this handbook can give you new insights for leadership. Whether you are working with an established youth group program or starting a new one, this book has loads of ideas for experiencing worship, creating community, and empowering mission. Whether the youth group is going well or facing tough problems, this book can help you build a better youth group.

41 Ways to Build a Better Youth Group is a handbook divided into four sections: Leadership, Worship, Community, and Mission. These four sections of ten chapters each cover almost every aspect of leading a youth group. In five to ten minutes, each chapter gives you practical ideas you can use at the next youth group gathering. If you are developing a job description for volunteer youth group leaders, turn to "Describe the Job." If youth want to talk about abortion, turn to "Handle Hot Topics." If new young people are moving into your community, turn to "Welcome Everyone." If youth are facing violence in their school and city, turn to "Seek Peace."

41 Ways to Build a Better Youth Group is based on the following assumptions:

1. The task of youth ministry is to provide opportunities that encourage youth to explore Christian faith, invite them to make a commitment, and disciple them to follow Jesus.
2. Youth alone must decide what they believe and what they will do. The youth group is a setting where Christian faith is presented to youth so they can make faith decisions.
3. Youth stand at many different places in relationship to Jesus Christ and the church, and those differences must be respected.
4. The lay volunteers who do most youth ministry in congregations care deeply about youth and nurturing their faith. These faithful people seek guidance in their ministry and can be trusted to fulfill that ministry as they are enabled by the Holy Spirit.

Each chapter opens with a story. All these stories are true.

The names, though changed, represent real people doing youth ministry with real youth groups. Countless young people have benefited from their faithfulness, and it has been my privilege, after fifteen years in youth ministry, to see some of these same young people become volunteer youth leaders themselves. Watching youth come to faith and seeing them become leaders in the church are among the greatest gifts of youth ministry. I offer this book with the prayer that it will make your job a little easier and equip you to do it more effectively as you enjoy the great honor of ministry with youth.

Michael Bogard
June 1995

C H A P T E R 1
BUILD A TEAM

When Jan began working with the youth at a suburban church, it seemed clear to her that the church needed to rethink its approach to youth ministry. In the past, most of the church's youth had come from church families. They knew the Bible, shared the same basic values, had a strong commitment to the church, and their best friends were other members of the youth group.

Not any more. The church's current crop of youth came from five cities and several cultures. Many didn't have church backgrounds. Their social life revolved not around the youth group, but around activities in the city and friends outside the youth group.

For all these reasons, the youth-group-centered approach to youth ministry that had been so effective in the past wasn't working the way it once had. Some parents expressed concern that their teens weren't as interested in church or as connected to church as they had been at that age.

Besides that, the youth seemed isolated from the rest of the congregation. It was almost as if there were two separate churches—the youth, and everybody else. The youth didn't feel like they were really part of the life of the church.

TOWARD A NEW MODEL OF MINISTRY

Jan had been reading *Blueprint for Congregational Youth Ministry* by Lavon Welty, and believed the integrated youth ministry model that Welty outlined could help the church address these needs. As a first step toward implementing that approach, Jan formed a youth ministry team.

Actually, a team was already taking shape. The lead pastor had started bringing together the junior youth sponsors,[*]

---

[*] The terms *youth sponsor* and *youth group leader* are used interchangeably throughout this book.

senior youth sponsors, youth Sunday school teachers, and mentoring coordinator so they could support each other in their ministries. Jan guided this group as it grew into more than a support group, as it became responsible for the joint planning and coordination of the church's total ministry with youth.

During their first two years together, the youth ministry team realized that having a full schedule of exciting activities was not the way to revitalize their youth ministry. Their youth already had lots of exciting activities to choose from, and the church would find it hard to compete successfully with them. So the team asked, "What can our church uniquely offer our youth?"

They came up with four answers:

1. Opportunity for peer relationships.
2. Opportunity for intergenerational relationships.
3. Opportunity for validation—to discover and use their gifts.
4. Opportunity to integrate faith and life.

These four goals, then, guided everything the youth ministry team did. The group went on to identify the various ministry settings in which these things happened, and evaluated which of these ministry settings were strong and which needed strengthening. The group also looked for ways to coordinate what was happening in the various ministry settings so that what was happening in Sunday school, for example, reinforced what was happening in youth group and other settings.

Once the group had grown into an effective team, Jan turned their attention to increasing congregational ownership of youth ministry. They worked together on ways to communicate their vision for youth ministry to the congregation. Individual team members looked for new ways to tie their particular ministries into the life of the rest of the church. Though no one could be sure exactly where all this would lead, a sense of anticipation was growing among youth ministry team members.

BUILDING YOUR TEAM

Almost any church's youth ministry will be stronger if those ministering with youth work together rather than separately. A youth ministry team can include:

- a pastoral team member whose responsibilities include youth ministry and catechism instruction;
- an elder or deacon (representing the congregation's board of elders or deacons);
- two parents of teens;
- two or three carefully selected youth;
- youth group leaders;
- youth Sunday school teachers;
- youth choir director;
- mentoring coordinator;
- any other leaders of youth ministry programs.

Youth and parents should choose their own representatives. Your congregation may also want to include representatives from the committee that oversees youth ministry, members from the congregation at large, or schoolteachers for their expertise and community awareness.

WHAT DOES THE TEAM DO?

The youth ministry team needs to meet together three times a year to guide, oversee, and evaluate the congregation's ministry with youth. Though the team may choose to do more, Welty suggests that its work should include at least the following seven tasks:

1. Determine youth needs.
2. Identify youth ministry settings.
3. Define the content and focus of the ministry in each setting.
4. Create a budget.
5. Support youth ministry leaders.
6. Evaluate the youth ministry program.
7. Report to the congregation.

If your church is starting a youth ministry team, you may want to do any or all of the following during your first meeting:

- Pray for God's guidance and for your youth and youth ministry leaders.
- Write a statement of purpose for your congregation's youth ministry.

- Write down the needs, interests, and concerns of your youth.
- Set goals for the coming year in the areas of worship, community, and mission.
- Assess your current youth ministry program.
- Begin developing a strategy for meeting your youth ministry goals.
- Enlist the services of those who can help reach those goals.
- Pray for God's blessing on your work.

Midway through the year, meet again to check your progress and make needed adjustments. At the end of your youth ministry year, meet a third time to evaluate your progress in relation to your goals.

TEAMWORK PAYS OFF

Now, six years after creating a youth ministry team, youth ministry at Jan's church is thriving again. The congregation has always cared about its youth, but they haven't always known how to express that caring. They now know specific ways to support their youth. They are more affirming of the youth, and youth and adults in the congregation interact more than ever before.

"AFTER A YEAR AND A HALF OF WORKING WITH A YOUTH MINISTRY TEAM, I CAN'T IMAGINE BEING WITHOUT ONE."

—Abe Bergen, *YouthGuide*, 2:3, p. 8

Youth ministry no longer revolves around youth group meetings as it once did. While youth group is still an important ministry setting, it meets no more than once a month, and other youth ministry settings have become more important. The youth have a growing sense that their contribution to the church matters. They know that the church cares about them as individuals, not just as a group.

Youth workers feel more supported than they did in the days before the team was formed. They know they have a place to bring their problems. And they are feeling more appreciated, both by other youth ministry team members and the congregation.

"We make a lot of decisions together," Jan says. "And we have a sense of being better able to meet the needs of youth, both in programming and pastoral care. We've found that together we can do more than we can separately."

Youth, youth workers, and congregation have all come out ahead because the church has adopted an integrated model of youth ministry led by a youth ministry team.

TEAM AS A FOUNDATIONAL STRUCTURE

Because of the many advantages of team ministry, the rest of this book is written with the assumption that your church's youth ministry is guided by a youth ministry team. If your church does not yet have such a team, forming one is probably the single most important step you can take to increase the effectiveness of your church's ministry with youth. Only after your team is in place will you be in a position to fully implement the other forty suggestions in this handbook.

PART 1

LEAD-
ER-
SHIP

CHAPTER 2
CREATE A VISION

Doug and Becky sat at their kitchen table in tears. They loved the youth. They enjoyed being with them. And they desperately wanted to see youth in their church know the Lord and serve the church. But everything seemed to be falling apart. Attendance at youth activities was sporadic. Petty rivalries were growing among the youth. No one wanted to pray or have a Bible study. And this year's service trip was fast becoming a resort vacation. Doug and Becky were frustrated and confused. They didn't know where they were going or where to turn. They were wondering if it was time to quit.

Too often, youth ministry leaders plunge in assuming that the church's ministry with youth should revolve around youth group activities. They move from event to event without clear expectations about what the events are intended to accomplish. Soon they tire of excuses, get frustrated by busyness, wonder about effectiveness, and begin to look forward to the end of their term—or they quit. Meanwhile, the youth lose their enthusiasm, complain about details, question the purpose, and begin wondering why they even participate. The root problem—lack of vision.

"WITHOUT A VISION, YOUTH MINISTRY IS BORING."

—Ridge Burns, *Create in Me a Youth Ministry*, p. 140

A vision statement defines what youth ministry is and why it is. It is the starting point for setting goals. It is the measuring point for evaluation. Whether creating a new youth ministry or evaluating an old one, defining a vision for youth ministry can provide a critically important focus. Vision can give new life to ministry with youth.

Throughout his ministry on earth, Jesus tried to help his disciples catch a vision of what God was trying to do, but the disciples had trouble getting it. From time to time they showed glimpses of insight as when Peter identified Jesus as the Messiah. Yet, in the end, Jesus had to spell it out so they knew exactly what he expected. "Go therefore and make disciples of all nations, baptizing them in the name of the Father and of the Son and of the Holy Spirit, and teaching them to obey everything that I have commanded you" (Matthew 28:19-20, New Revised Standard Version).

A biblical vision for youth ministry must grow out of Jesus' vision. A simple vision statement could be: youth ministry invites youth to faith in Jesus Christ and disciples them to follow Jesus Christ. This statement focuses two questions: to whom do we minister and how will we minister? The many answers to those questions become the purposes, goals, and strategies for fulfilling the vision.

Here's one way to define a vision for ministry with youth, then move forward to make it reality.

STEP 1: DRAFT A VISION STATEMENT.

Begin by calling a "visioning" meeting of all of those involved in ministry with youth: the pastor, worship planners, youth group leaders, youth choir director, Sunday school teachers, parent and youth representatives, and others connected to the congregation's youth ministry. Begin the meeting with a Bible study on the nature and mission of the church. Then form smaller groups of two or three to begin formulating a vision statement. Make this assignment: "Using your own words, create a one- or two-sentence statement of our congregation's vision for ministry with youth that grows out of Jesus' vision." Gather the large group, share statements, and then combine them into one statement everyone can support. Or, invite groups of two to join into groups of four and combine their vision statements into one all can support. Then combine the groups of four into groups of eight and again combine their statements into one. Both of these methods will take time, but they should result in a concise vision statement that reflects everyone's thinking and enjoys everyone's support.

STEP 2: IDENTIFY THE SETTINGS FOR MINISTRY WITH YOUTH.

Many congregations have the youth group setting and the Sunday school setting, but there are more. Catechism or confirmation is a youth ministry setting. Sunday morning worship and other aspects of congregational life are youth ministry settings. Families are youth ministry settings. Service and mission events and formal and informal mentoring are youth ministry settings. And some churches have youth ministry settings uniquely their own. When identifying youth ministry settings, keep in mind that your congregation can minister with two groups of youth, those in the church and those outside the church.

STEP 3: IMPLEMENT THE VISION.

This is a time for raising questions. How does this setting share faith? How does it disciple faith? How do we teach or worship in this setting? How does this setting relate to youth within the church? to youth outside the church? How does this setting build relationships among the youth and relationships with the church? This is the step for imagining goals, plans, programs, curriculums, events, activities, and strategies. This is where the vision becomes a plan.

STEP 4: IMPLEMENT THE PLAN.

Decide what you can and will do. Budget, time, and the availability of workers will all be limiting factors. Remember that it is okay to start small and plan to do more in the future. It may be helpful to create a chart with a column for each setting on the top and a row for each month of the year on the left side. The intersecting grid provides space to record plans and activities so that you have a visual picture of how the vision for youth ministry will be implemented.

Your vision statement should guide not only your planning but also your evaluation. Every element of your youth ministry, from every setting to every program and activity, should serve that vision. When every person involved knows and understands that vision and is focused on fulfilling it, then God's Spirit can move in ways that touch the lives of youth and bring them into the kingdom.

CHAPTER 3
LOVE THE GROUP

Colleen and Josh thoroughly enjoyed their ministry as youth group leaders with the three youth in their church. They met as a group every two months for an outing. Between these gatherings, Colleen and Josh made it a point to talk to the youth every Sunday. On occasion they taught the youth Sunday school class and attended important events in the lives of their youth.

Ben and Christina worked as youth group leaders with a group of twenty-eight grade 10-12 youth. They and the youth group met every Wednesday night for Bible study and every other Sunday evening for worship, discussion of an important issue, and snacks. Along with two other couples and a youth executive cabinet, Ben and Christina also helped give leadership to an extensive youth ministry program including service trips, denominational conferences, youth-led worship services once every three months, and a peer ministry training program.

Even though these two youth groups and their programs were very different, each youth sponsor team enjoyed an exciting and fruitful youth ministry. The key for both youth

"LOVE IS THE

SECRET INGREDIENT."

—Joan Sturkie, *Listening with Love*, p. 11

groups was volunteers who loved the youth and loved their ministry with the youth group. Colleen and Josh and Ben and Christina had discovered the most important key to effective youth group ministry.

When love motivates ministry, the exact answers to the questions youth sponsors most often ask become less important. Since no two youth groups are alike, no two youth group ministries will be alike. Even from one year to the next, the church's youth group will change as new youth enter and older youth leave. Loving youth and youth ministry, then, is the glue that keeps youth group leaders and youth connected as the youth group changes.

QUESTION 1: WHAT IS THE IDEAL YOUTH GROUP SIZE?

There is no ideal size. Both large and small groups have their advantages. Large groups allow:

- different program options because not all youth group experiences have to include every person;
- the involvement of several adults;
- some worship, community, and mission options that require a larger number of people.

Small groups allow:

- flexibility, informality, and spur-of-the-moment changes;
- intimacy and deep friendships because fewer youth are involved;
- involvement of all the youth in planning and leadership since there is little need for formal organization.

QUESTION 2: HOW OFTEN SHOULD THE YOUTH GROUP MEET?

There is no magic number of youth group meetings. Every group needs to determine the schedule of meetings that best serves its goals and vision for youth ministry. In determining the number of youth group meetings, keep a few realities in mind:

- *Youth are busy.* The schedules of youth must be respected because they usually have little control over much of their schedules. At the same time, sponsors can help youth set priorities, evaluate their interests, and set before them the challenge to allow Jesus Christ to be first in their lives.
- *Meet for meaning.* Getting together just to get together is no longer acceptable for most youth. They need good reasons to meet. Involving youth in the process of determining meeting frequency and the reasons for meeting gives them ownership and a greater commitment to youth group meetings.
- *Break with tradition.* Many youth are willing to meet at times

other than the traditional Wednesday and Sunday evenings. Work and school schedules may better lend themselves to lunch, Saturday morning, or Monday afternoon meetings. Make room for meetings that don't have to include everyone. If they have enough opportunities to get together, youth won't mind if they miss now and then.

QUESTION 3: WHAT SHOULD THE YOUTH GROUP DO?

The focus of ministry with youth should be on building relationships with youth rather than on doing things with youth. Most young people long for an adult to be trustworthy, honest, caring, and faithful. Jesus exemplified this ministry of relationship. His first interest was always the person.

Although building relationships is the primary focus of youth group ministry, youth groups do things together. When asking what the youth group should do, keep in mind three ministry areas. In all that the youth group does, it should seek for a balance among these three:

- **Worship** emphasizes the relationship Christians have with God through Jesus Christ. It can take the form of Bible study, prayer, discipleship discussions, spiritual life retreats, or worship services. In worship, youth are invited to love God or express their love for God.

- **Community** emphasizes the relationship Christians have with one another. Community means showing how love, concern, compassion, caring, and encouragement is given to one another. Playing games, building friendships, attending conferences, and working in the congregation are ways youth experience community. In community-building, youth are invited to love one another.

- **Mission** emphasizes the relationship Christians have with the world. Mission experiences can include mission trips, service projects, evangelism, or peace and justice advocacy, in which youth learn to see the world as the object of God's love. In doing mission, youth learn to love the world the way God loves the world.

Whether the group is large or small, whether it meets once a month or once a week, whether it prays together or plays together, youth sponsors can love the youth they work with. Inviting youth to faith in Jesus Christ and discipling youth through worship, community, and mission grow out of that basic relationship. Loving youth and youth ministry, therefore, does not depend on the size of the youth group, how often it meets, or what it does; it depends on the youth group leader's willingness to respond to God's love with love for others, with love for youth.

YOUTH MINISTRY

A BLUEPRINT FOR BUILDING A BETTER YOUTH GROUP

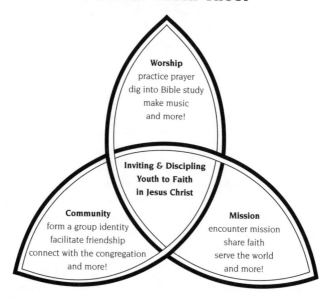

Worship
practice prayer
dig into Bible study
make music
and more!

**Inviting & Discipling
Youth to Faith
in Jesus Christ**

Community
form a group identity
facilitate friendship
connect with the congregation
and more!

Mission
encounter mission
share faith
serve the world
and more!

Leadership

Youth   **Youth Ministry Team**   **Youth Leaders**

CHAPTER 4
DESCRIBE THE JOB

Lavonne and Harv were clear that their role as youth sponsors involved only being at the youth group meetings and chaperoning the youth events. Gwen and Stan, on the other hand, led Bible studies, visited schools, sent birthday cards, and prayed every day for the youth in their group. When Marcia began her term as a youth sponsor, she didn't know what she was supposed to do. And nobody in the church seemed to be able to tell her.

Lavonne and Harv were both involved in other areas of the congregation's life. Harv was a deacon and Lavonne taught second-grade Sunday school. They both worked full time and they had four children, two in elementary school. Lavonne and Harv were giving to youth ministry all the time and energy they could afford.

Gwen and Stan were recently married, had no children, but spent a lot of time with youth at camps and at church. Stan worked outside the home, Gwen was a committed gardener, and both were dedicated to a simple lifestyle. Gwen and Stan had more time and energy they could give to youth ministry.

Marcia, single and building her career, was new to the congregation. Because she cared about youth and cared about the church, she said yes when she was asked to be a youth sponsor, even though she wasn't sure what it would involve. Her uncertainty turned to confusion after she talked first with Lavonne and Harv, then with Gwen and Stan. Which couple was right? Or were they both right? And how was she to know what was the right role for her?

Many people agree to be youth sponsors only to be left on their own to discover what they are supposed to do. Previous and current sponsors, parents, pastors, and others in the congregation may all have different ideas of what youth sponsors do. As these ideas become expectations, the new youth sponsor can feel trapped. A job description for the role of volunteer youth sponsor can help your church avoid this trap. Here is one way to develop one.

STEP 1: DEFINE THE PRIMARY PURPOSE OF THE GROUP.

Call together those involved in your congregation's total youth ministry program. With your congregation's vision statement for youth ministry in mind, review or define the goals of the youth group. A youth group can function as a social gathering, a Bible study group, an outreach program, or a combination of these. All are good reasons for youth to meet, but they do require different roles for adult sponsors.

If the youth group meets for social reasons, adult sponsors may function as coordinators and as an adult presence. If your group meets for Bible study, the adult sponsors may need gifts for facilitating discussion of Scripture. Many groups look for adult sponsors who can fulfill several roles. The key is to first define the primary purpose of the group so you can define the role of the adult sponsors.

STEP 2: AFFIRM A RELATIONAL STYLE OF LEADERSHIP.

The role of youth sponsors is similar to Jesus' role with his disciples. The Emmaus story in Luke 24 offers the model of a leader who walks alongside and listens, raises significant and open-ended questions, offers guidance and teaching, and invites commitment and growth. Style of leadership is often more important than the task of leadership. Youth remember who you are more than what you do.

STEP 3: DRAFT A JOB DESCRIPTION.

Draw up a worksheet with the six headings listed below, then break into small groups and ask each group to fill out the worksheet. When they are done, call the groups together to report. Then, with a fresh worksheet on the board, refine all the ideas into one realistic job description.

I. *Qualifications*. Some qualities will be obvious. Youth sponsors care about youth and enjoy being with youth. They are committed to Jesus Christ and the mission of the church. Other expectations can be more flexible: their gender and age, their particular talents and gifts, whether they are single or married. Some churches may also need to address whether official church membership is required.

"BEING A VOLUNTEER YOUTH SPONSOR IS AN HONOR!"

—Norma Peters Duerksen,
minister with youth

II. *Tasks.* Defining the specific tasks of youth sponsors can be extremely helpful in clarifying expectations. Possible tasks might include:

A. With the youth executive, plan two Sunday evening meetings per month.

B. Accompany the youth group on one extended trip per year.

C. Arrange transportation to the denominational conference.

D. Attend one training event per year.

The specific tasks outlined in the job description will depend on factors specific to each group such as size, purpose and goals, frequency of activities, and number of sponsors.

III. *Time.* Every volunteer deserves to know how much time the job may require. Some sponsors can give more time than others, but a reasonable range should be defined so the sponsor knows what to expect. Include the time needed for service trips, weekend retreats, and conferences.

IV. *Cost.* Youth ministry costs money as well as time. Teaching, attending events, and accompanying youth on trips can cost the youth sponsor money. Ideally, the church should provide a budget to cover these expenses. If the church has no youth ministry budget, an estimate of these expenses can help the sponsor know what to expect.

V. *Resources.* A budget can provide funds for media resources, guest presenters, and all the other necessary "stuff" for youth ministry. Also list other resources available to youth sponsors.

Quick Tip
YOUTH SPONSOR TERMS

Many volunteer youth sponsors wonder how long they should stay in the job. One rule might be: as long as you are excited and effective. But a more logical answer might be to determine the length of term based on natural transitions. Two years is a minimum, but it is often too short. Most youth sponsors feel it takes a year to learn the ropes and get to know the youth. Once you have gone to all that work, it gets easier, especially if the load is shared among a group of youth sponsors.

A grade 9-12 youth group might call for four-year terms so the sponsor can walk through the high school experience with one class. A grade 10-12 youth group might call for three-year terms. A grade 7-12 group might also suggest three-year terms since most will not commit to six years. However you decide, if you let natural transitions guide you, youth will more readily understand the transitions of youth sponsors as they adjust to their own transitions.

Church libraries, conference and denominational resource centers, youth ministry organizations, and training events all help the youth sponsor realize help is available for the job. Many youth sponsors will accept a loose job description if they know where to go to find help and answers to their questions.

VI. *Accountability.* Of all the elements of a job description, this may be the most important because it defines who carries the responsibility for the church's youth ministry program. Whether it is the pastor, a youth ministry team, a committee, or the deacons/elders, someone other than the youth sponsors should oversee the youth ministry program. This allows the youth sponsors to focus on building relationships with the youth, and lets others set policies, mediate conflicts, determine priorities, and give direction. The youth sponsor's job description should include periodic meetings with the supervisory person or group.

STEP 4: LEAVE SOME FLEXIBILITY.

Job descriptions should never be set in stone. They need to be specific enough to let people know expectations, but flexible enough to allow for individual differences, talents, and gifts. The role of youth sponsor should leave room for Harv and Lavonne, Stan and Gwen, and Marcia.

Each congregation must work out its own youth sponsor's job description because specifics depend on current structures for congregational life, available financial resources, and the congregation's vision for youth ministry. One of the bonuses of developing a job description is that the process can itself generate new interest and enthusiasm for youth ministry. And as clear expectations replace confusion, it may become much easier to find those elusive volunteer youth sponsors.

YOUTH GROUP LEADER
JOB DESCRIPTION WORKSHEET

1. **Qualifications**
    - _____
    - _____
    - _____

2. **Tasks**
    - _____
    - _____
    - _____
    - _____
    - _____

3. **Time** _____ per week

4. **Cost** _____ per month

5. **Resources available**
    - _____
    - _____
    - _____
    - _____
    - _____

6. **Accountability**
    - _____
    - _____

CHAPTER 5
PLAN THE YEAR

Teresa had been chosen. Encouraged by many in her congregation, tapped on the shoulder by her pastor, requested by the youth group, invited by the other youth sponsors: Teresa had been chosen. Now she was a new youth sponsor facing incredible expectations. Everyone believed Teresa was the person who would fix the youth ministry in her church. And she did!

Teresa's gift? She was an organizer. Her church's youth ministry was nearly extinct. There were few youth meetings, rare youth activities, and no youth trips. The entire congregation realized they needed someone with vision and the skills to carry out the vision. Teresa had been chosen.

> **"WHEN THERE IS**
>
> **NO MORE FAITH**
>
> **IN THE FUTURE, THERE IS**
>
> **NO POWER IN THE PRESENT."**
>
> —John Dawson, "Developing Leadership in Youth, Part Two," *Youthful Info*

Chapter 2 addressed the need for vision in congregational youth ministry and described a process for defining vision. Once a vision for youth ministry is defined, the next process is planning youth ministry within each youth ministry setting. For Teresa, that meant planning a year of youth ministry with the youth group.

STEP 1: CALL A PLANNING MEETING.

This meeting will include everyone concerned about youth ministry in the youth group—the youth sponsors and the youth. It may also include parent representatives, other members of the youth ministry team, and the pastor or youth pastor. In this meeting the entire year will be planned.

STEP 2: DEVELOP GOALS.

What specific outcomes do you want to see by the end of the year that will move you toward fulfilling your congregation's stated vision for youth ministry? Write these goals around the three ministry areas of worship, community, and mission, perhaps setting a certain number of goals in each area, such as three for worship, three for community, and three for mission. It may also be helpful to break into groups of three or four persons with each group working on a different ministry area. If you do break into small groups, come together after a set time, ask each group to share its work, and then invite response from the larger group. Through this step it is important to remember that goals are temporary. They don't have to be exact and they don't have to last forever.

STEP 3: BRAINSTORM POSSIBLE ACTIVITIES.

What programs and activities will the youth group experience to achieve the goals you have set for the coming year? One helpful way to generate ideas is through brainstorming. Brainstorming involves two parts. First is the process of getting the ideas. It begins with throwing out ideas and writing them all down. Second is the process of sorting through the ideas. The acronym BRAINSTORM can help us remember the process.

Part 1: Get the ideas.

B ombard the air with ideas. This is the moment of abandon when people throw out one idea after another.

R eceive every idea regardless of how feasible it may seem. Someone's wild idea may generate a more practical idea.

A bandon criticism. Criticism of any idea tends to cut off the flow. Criticism includes negative comments, laughing, and groans.

I nvite ideas from each person present so that everyone contributes to the process. This means soliciting ideas from quieter participants.

N ote on newsprint everything that is suggested. You may also want to record the brainstorming session on tape so that no idea is lost.

Part 2: Sort the ideas.

S ort the ideas by categories using three sheets of newsprint, one each for *worship*, *community*, and *mission*.

T ag the favorite ideas with a plus sign, and leave the rest as options. Every idea is an option, though all may not be possible right now.

O rder the tagged ideas by priority according to schedule, available resources, cost, and feasibility.

R ecommend the ideas you wish to try in the coming year and put them on the planning work sheet.

M ove. Begin putting the ideas into action.

STEP 4: SCHEDULE THE ACTIVITIES.

Once the ideas have been placed into categories, create a planning work sheet with each month or every week of the coming year in rows on the left side, and put worship, community, and mission along the top in three columns. Then, using the brainstorming lists, begin to plug in the programs, activities, trips, curriculums, and events the youth group will experience over the course of the coming year. When you have finished, you will have planned the whole year!

If your youth group does not have a youth sponsor like Teresa, or even if you do, you might want to try setting up leadership teams of two to three people who will follow through on coordinating each experience. These teams, which can include both adults and youth, check schedules, secure facilities, gather resources, invite, lead, and follow up the experience. This method takes some of the pressure off the youth sponsor and hands over leadership to others.

STEP 5: EVALUATE EACH YOUTH GROUP EXPERIENCE.

After each activity, participants and leaders can reflect on whether the experience met the stated goals. Practical issues can also be evaluated. Were there enough resources? How effective were they? Were the time and timing appropriate? Who came and why? Who did not come and why? What worked and what didn't? Notes taken during these evaluations will be helpful for the final step.

STEP 6: EVALUATE THE YEAR.

At the end of the year, schedule another meeting of the planning team and evaluate the total youth group experience for the past year. Be prepared to hand out brief summaries of the evaluations of individual activities so the meeting can move more quickly. When the evaluation process is completed, make recommendations for the coming year that the new year's planning team can consider. Recognize, however, that recommendations are not commandments. Needs, goals, and hopes will be different, and some recommendations based on the past year may not suit the new year.

Not everyone needs or likes this kind of precise planning, but for many, this approach can lead to a youth group experience that is more balanced, more purposeful, and more effective in achieving the church's goals for its ministry with youth.

YOUTH GROUP
VISION, GOALS, & PLANNING WORKSHEET

Primary Purpose or Vision Statement:

_____

_____

_____

Goals:

Worship

• _____

• _____

• _____

Community

• _____

• _____

• _____

Mission

• _____

• _____

• _____

ACTICITY PLANNER	WORSHIP	COMMUNITY	MISSION
January			
February			
March			
April			
May			
June			
July			
August			
September			
October			
November			
December			

CHAPTER 6
PARTNER WITH YOUR PASTOR

At one of their youth ministry team planning meetings, Tim and Judy presented a big idea. They wanted to take the youth group on a service trip to the city for an "urban encounter." They had made inquiries about lodging, service, learning opportunities, estimated costs, and travel. When they presented their idea, their pastor was visibly excited. She enthusiastically encouraged the idea with the congregation and offered her support to the sponsors and the youth group at every opportunity. When the time came for the trip, Tim and Judy and the youth group had the

> **"MOST PASTORS**
>
> **BELIEVE IN**
>
> **YOUTH MINISTRY."**
>
> —Doug Stevens, "Looking over Both Sides of the Fence," *Youthworker*, 2:3, p. 25

prayers, the funds, and the best wishes of the entire congregation. Their pastor had been a key player in the project.

Often youth sponsors have great ideas, but don't know where to go with them. Partnering with your pastor can be the key. Tim and Judy had taken several steps with their idea that won their pastor's enthusiastic support. Those steps grew out of several appropriate assumptions they had made:

ASSUMPTION 1: YOUTH ARE A PART OF YOUR PASTOR'S CONGREGATION, TOO!

Though only a few pastors are immersed in youth ministry, almost all pastors want their ministries to include youth, although they depend on others in the congregation to carry most of the load of youth ministry. It is important to acknowledge that both kinds of pastors see the youth as a part of their ministries. Your job is to complement your pastor's involvement in youth ministry so that you and your pastor are working as an effective team.

ASSUMPTION 2: PASTORS USUALLY SUPPORT THOSE WHO DO THEIR HOMEWORK.

The decision-makers in your congregation need good information to make good decisions. To alleviate these folks' fears and assure them that you know what you are doing, work out as many details as possible before presenting an idea. In Tim and Judy's case, their pastor became a key supporter of their idea partly because it didn't create a lot of work for her. It is easy for pastors like Tim and Judy's to be supportive when youth sponsors take the initiative and show that they know what they are doing. Right or wrong, many pastors are less supportive if it looks like they will have to be deeply involved in the planning process.

Quick Tip
PARTNERING WITH THE PASTOR
(FOR YOUTH AND SPONSORS)

1. Get to know your pastor.
2. Send your pastor birthday cards.
3. Use your pastor as a guest resource person.
4. Consult with your pastor when planning a youth-led worship service.
5. Invite your pastor to a youth activity.
6. Give your pastor a night on the town either with a gift certificate, free baby-sitting, or both.
7. Give your pastor an award.
8. Update your pastor; listen to an album or watch a movie together.
9. Prepare a list of sermon themes or issues that interest the youth group.
10. Send your pastor to a youth ministry training event.

ASSUMPTION 3: IT'S OKAY TO OCCASIONALLY INVITE YOUR PASTOR'S PARTICIPATION.

Youth groups can become like a little church within the church. If the pastor has not been involved in the youth group, he or she may not feel welcome to participate in youth activities without being specifically invited. If your youth hardly know their pastor, this may be the reason. Or, the pastor may just be too busy. Either way, invite your pastor to join the youth from time to time so relationships can develop and your pastor's interest in the youth can grow, and so the youth will see the pastor as an important adult in their lives.

ASSUMPTION 4: IT'S IMPORTANT TO BE CONSISTENT WITH YOUR CHURCH'S VALUES AND BELIEFS.

Not every idea or event that is popular with youth fits with how a congregation understands its mission. Pastors, who are responsible for giving focus to the congregation's mission, are acutely aware of this. If you want the support and cooperation of your pastor, it is important to be sure your vision for the youth group is consistent with the congregation's vision, consulting with your pastor if you are in doubt. Working at this issue beforehand can prevent problems and generate support.

ASSUMPTION 5: THERE ARE TIMES WHEN THE PASTOR CAN ONLY HELP A LITTLE.

Pastors have limits on what and how much they can do. Schedule conflicts, health, physical ability, lack of knowledge and understanding about youth and youth ministry, previous history, size and age of the congregation—all are factors that may influence the pastor's availability to be involved with youth. It is important to recognize how much involvement is reasonable to expect from your pastor. Limited involvement does not mean the pastor doesn't care. Tim and Judy's pastor may not have been able to do any more than support their idea, but this turned out to be a big help.

Enlisting your pastor's support in youth ministry can go a long way to gaining greater congregational support and encouragement for youth ministry.

CHAPTER 7
DEVELOP YOUTH LEADERSHIP

During Chris's senior year he developed a new set of friends who were leading him down a road to self-destruction. He began experimenting with alcohol and drugs and letting go of positive friendships and activities. Although he was still kind, gentle, and thoughtful, a hard edge was beginning to show.

Chris wasn't happy about where he was headed, but he felt overwhelmed by his friends and his need for their acceptance, unable to change direction on his own. Hoping to exert a positive influence, I invited Chris to spend the summer at camp. I hoped it would give him a chance to sort through his life and think about the decisions he was making.

At first Chris worked in maintenance, but through the summer his role changed. Chris got more involved with the kids. As he watched the staff and attended orientation sessions, Chris's interest in counseling grew. When he finally asked if he could be a counselor, I knew he was ready. He enjoyed being with kids, he was compassionate, and he could talk about his own faith struggles and the positive, life-changing decisions he was making to follow Christ. By the end of the summer, Chris was a confident counselor and we had confidence in him.

> **"THE** YOUTH
>
> **WORKER'S PRIMARY**
>
> **ROLE IS TO INVOLVE**
>
> **YOUTH IN THEIR OWN YOUTH MINISTRY."**
>
> —Thom & Joani Schultz, *Kids Taking Charge: Youth Led Youth Ministry*, p. 14

As youth pass through adolescence, they work through a whole series of questions. They ask, "Who am I?" In their search for the answer they may try different clothing or hairstyles. Sometimes they assert their growing sense of independence by questioning voices of authority. Often youth isolate themselves as they wage an inner struggle.

Youth also ask, "What can I do?" As they look for answers, they may jump from one activity to another, trying the possibilities and testing their potential. Or, they may completely devote themselves to one thing to see how good they can get.

Finally, youth begin to define their allegiance by asking the question, "Whose am I?" To answer this question, youth go exploring. They raise difficult questions. They open their minds to alternative ideas. They try on different beliefs. They may make commitments, but rarely are they lifelong decisions.

All youth, Chris included, go through this process, and it is through this process that leadership can be developed in youth. Attentive youth sponsors can guide youth through their questions and provide learning opportunities, all the while believing in them and empowering them to lead.

STEP 1: PROVIDE TRAINING FOR YOUTH LEADERSHIP.

Leadership skills are not innate; they must be learned. From planning activities to making announcements, from taking minutes to preparing a presentation, from welcoming guests to comforting a friend, leadership skills must be learned. Youth sponsors can play a key role in insuring the teaching of leadership skills.

Learning leadership skills can happen informally. One excellent model has four simple stages:

Stage 1: "I do it, and you watch."
Stage 2: "We do it together."
Stage 3: "You do it, and I watch."
Stage 4: "You do it on your own."

Too often, when youth are given leadership roles, they are expected to start at stage four on the assumption that youth know what to do. But in developing youth leadership, it is essential that youth sponsors go through each stage. Stage one may have already occurred, but don't just assume it has; make certain.

Leadership skills can also be learned in more formal ways. Taking youth to youth leadership training events, using a leadership training curriculum with the youth group, or partnering youth with adult leaders in the church for a period of time can all be part of the training process.

STEP 2: PROVIDE OPPORTUNITIES FOR LEADERSHIP.

The first place to do this, of course, is the youth group. A youth executive committee provides the best opportunity for youth to lead. These youth can run meetings, brainstorm ideas, help make decisions, implement activities, evaluate, and re-imagine new possibilities.

But the youth group setting offers other leadership opportunities, too. Youth can lead worship, music, and prayer. Searching, studying, and evaluating resources not only gives youth the opportunity to learn from the experiences of others, but it also stimulates their own ideas. Developing prayer teams, providing refreshments, creating a newsletter, making contacts, inviting friends, and participating in service actions are all opportunities for leadership. Through these opportunities, youth learn and cultivate leadership skills. By rotating leadership roles through the year, you can offer these opportunities to more youth.

> Help a youth become a **big TOE** in the Body of Christ
>
> **T** - Training
> **O** - Opportunities
> **E** - Empowerment

The church also offers tremendous opportunities for youth leadership beyond the youth group. Youth can participate in leadership in almost every aspect of congregational life, including choirs, Sunday school, committees, worship, and summer Bible school. Youth sponsors can be the advocates to the church for involving youth in these areas. An excellent way for

Quick Tip
WHEN YOUTH FAIL

1. Let them.
2. Meet to discuss the failure.
3. Restate the expectations.
4. Define the failure.
5. Outline the consequences.
6. Develop successful strategies to succeed.
7. Choose a successful strategy.
8. Develop a new opportunity.
9. Remind, remind, remind.
10. Celebrate success.

youth to learn leadership is by "shadowing," learning as they watch and help adult leaders.

Finally, many opportunities for leadership development occur in settings outside the congregation. Camps, conference youth events, and denominational youth organizations usually have to beat the bushes to find youth interested in helping in leadership roles. Youth sponsors can encourage youth to take advantage of these opportunities to learn by doing.

STEP 3: EMPOWER YOUTH FOR LEADERSHIP.

The most common complaint youth have about leadership is their sense that few adults believe they can do it. But the fact is, *youth can lead*, and youth sponsors can help make it happen. First, youth sponsors can intentionally advocate for youth leadership. This may involve speaking to church leaders about involving youth in leadership. It may mean working to change church structures, such as membership requirements, that hinder youth leadership. It may mean lobbying for financial support to train youth leaders.

Second, the youth sponsors can encourage youth in their leadership positions. Giving reminders, sending cards of encouragement, inviting reports, encouraging peer support, and praying are little acts that feel big to youth.

Third, youth sponsors can hold youth accountable. When youth lead, they can learn that leadership is a responsibility that cannot be neglected. They learn that people depend on them. They learn that successful leadership brings rewards, and failed leadership has consequences. Just as youth need opportunities to succeed at leadership, they must also be allowed to fail. Intervening to avert failure is appropriate only if the consequences will be truly hurtful to others.

Through his summer at camp, Chris made some decisions about who he was, what he could do, and to whom he belonged. Given the opportunity, a few skills, and the assurance that he could do the job, Chris then became an important leader in the lives of kids at camp. Although he did not change the whole world, he did change his world.

Youth can lead!

CHAPTER 8
ANTICIPATE THE CHALLENGES

Ed and Anna had enjoyed tremendous success with their youth group. Beginning with seven youth, their group had grown to eighteen. Youth were bringing friends. Other youth were coming in response to door-to-door invitations in the neighborhood. And their congregation's ministry to parents had brought new youth into the group.

The challenge? Many of these youth came from families in trauma. Some were confronting their own drug and alcohol addiction. And others were fringe youth, alienated in their high schools, but finding acceptance in the church.

Most youth groups today include youth facing similar situations. Whether it is abuse, poor choices, family tragedies, or difficult circumstances, life for many teens today includes serious challenges. Helping youth cope with these challenges does not require professional counseling skills. Anyone who is ALERT to five principles can be a people-helper.

PRINCIPLE 1: ACCEPT.

Jesus' ability to help people grew as much out of his acceptance of them as from his miraculous power. His greatest gift was his unconditional love. Ministry with youth requires this gift of acceptance.

Youth sponsors accept youth by recognizing their needs. This can be done by learning to know their families, asking about school, and attending an occasional event. Youth sponsors can pay attention to the interests and social experiences of youth. They can respectfully get acquainted with the youth culture so they can with integrity affirm what is good in it and challenge what is not good.

Youth sponsors can accept that youth are still learning and growing. Youth make poor choices that have painful consequences, but bad things also happen to them that they cannot control. In either case, youth sponsors can help youth pick up the pieces and learn from their experiences. Youth experience the gift of God's love through youth sponsors who display it in their lives.

PRINCIPLE 2: LISTEN.

Youth often have no voice. Most of their lives are controlled by others who rarely ask for their input. Before youth offer their opinions or ideas, adults have often already decided what will be done. When youth bare their souls, too many adults are quick to deny them their feelings.

Youth sponsors can give youth a voice by listening to their ideas and opinions. Youth have tremendous potential for creativity and problem solving. Providing forums, taking polls, conducting surveys, asking for evaluation, and empowering youth for leadership are ways to recognize what youth have to offer.

Youth sponsors can also alertly listen to the fear, pain, and tragedy in the lives of youth. Many young people are facing adult problems with a child's life experience. Although most youth sponsors are not prepared to be counselors, they can be caring friends who listen as young people tell their stories. They can give young people information that can help them face their problems. And youth sponsors can walk with young people as they confront and overcome their problems.

PRINCIPLE 3: ENCOURAGE.

In our society, youth are constantly reminded of their inadequacy. Media, societal expectations, and even many families are constantly pointing out the failures of youth. In response, the old adage "it takes ten positives to overcome one negative" can be a prophetic call to youth sponsors.

Encourage youth by catching them doing right. Even something simple like being on time for a youth group meeting can be an opportunity for praise. Graduations, service projects, volunteer work, and accomplishments can all provide opportunities for celebrating the good things youth do.

Encourage youth by being just and gracious. Every youth group will face discipline issues. It is important, therefore, to be clear about expectations and consequences. When these are clear, most youth can accept just responses to their attitudes and behaviors. When those just responses are tempered by grace, youth will often be awed and motivated to new levels of faithful living.

PRINCIPLE 4: RESPECT.

Respect is a catchword among many youth today. They want people to respect who they are and what they can do. They want to be treated as adults, not as children. They want the power to control what happens to them. Unfortunately, many adults have no respect for youth, and many youth seek respect through inappropriate means.

Youth sponsors can respect youth by treating them as young people becoming adults. Youth often get caught between

> **"FOR** SOME
>
> **TROUBLED YOUTH,**
>
> **YOU MAY BE THE**
>
> **ONLY GOOD MODEL THEY HAVE."**
>
> —Dwight Spotts and David Veerman,
> *Reaching Out to Troubled Youth,* p. 68

conflicting signals. A fifteen-year-old is old enough to drive, but not old enough to vote. A thirteen-year-old is old enough to get pregnant, but not old enough to drink alcohol. When faced with such ambiguities, youth generally give themselves the advantage of the doubt. Youth sponsors can help young people live with the gray areas of adolescence.

Youth sponsors can respect youth by cherishing who they are, celebrating what they can do, and advocating for them to uncaring or disrespectful adults. Youth do make important contributions in their families, churches, and communities. Youth sponsors can model respect and admiration as well as invite that respect from others.

PRINCIPLE 5: TEACH.

Many youth lack the tools to make right choices. Because there is no longer a moral consensus in our society, many youth never learn moral values, nor do they learn the tools for developing them. Many adults assume that children and youth are picking up moral values on their own. Many parents and adults believe six- to sixteen-year-olds are capable of making wise choices about decisions with lifelong consequences. Most cannot.

Youth sponsors can teach youth how to develop a system of moral values. Youth are willing to hear about issues of morality—what is right and wrong—if they are given the freedom to think, evaluate, and decide.

Youth sponsors can teach youth to anticipate both the good and bad consequences of their choices. Youth can learn that most choices have several consequences, some more far-reaching than others. As youth learn these realities, they are more likely to avoid choices with negative consequences. Youth sponsors also need to be careful to respond to youth's poor choices proportionately. Bringing beer to a retreat and tearing a page in the hymnal are both poor choices, but one can have far more serious consequences than the other. Ministry with youth *will* bring challenges. There is no cure-all solution to any one of those difficult moments. But applying these principles can help youth face the tough challenges in their lives.

CHAPTER 9
INVOLVE PARENTS

Steve and Cindy provide enthusiastic leadership to the youth group. Along with Bill and Kris, these youth sponsors have been developing a core of youth who are taking leadership of meetings and events. Unfortunately, attendance has not improved and both the sponsors and the involved youth are frustrated by the lack of participation. A major reason for low participation seems to be that many of the youth's parents simply are not encouraging them to take part in the youth group.

Many youth sponsors identify lack of parental support as their biggest frustration. Most youth sponsors and church leaders assume that parents will automatically support the youth ministry program and help to make it a priority in the lives of their youth. Then reality hits. Youth don't show up. Parents make excuses. And youth sponsors get frustrated.

Why does this happen? Often it's because some parents feel the church is not sensitive to their needs or the needs of their family. There can be several reasons for this:

Reason 1: Many churches assume the traditional nuclear family as the norm when, in fact, there are more and more single-parent, blended, multigenerational, and other "nontraditional" families.

Reason 2: Many families put the church and its activities low on their time-priority list.

Reason 3: Too many churches are failing to speak in contemporary terms to contemporary issues. Many families, and youth in particular, find worship and congregational life irrelevant and boring.

Although there are no guarantees, youth sponsors who become sensitive to these realities may find more parents becoming their allies.

Three basic principles can help turn parents into supporters of the youth group program. **Communication** is the most important; parents need to know what is going on. **Involvement,** inviting parents into the youth group program, can help them to feel ownership of the program and provide opportunities for their input. **Sensitivity** to family life and family decisions will help avoid conflicts and make youth ministry more relevant. Perhaps some of the following ideas can help you build stronger relationships with parents:

COMMUNICATION:

Step 1. Learn to know the parents of the youth.
- Take the initiative to greet them on Sunday mornings.
- Call them on the phone and meet for a snack.
- Write a letter introducing yourself and your goals and plans for the coming youth ministry year.
- Invite them for dinner and begin a friendship.

Step 2. Invite parent input in youth ministry planning.
- Hold a brainstorming planning meeting for parents.
- Ask for family schedules for the coming year.
- Sponsor a fall retreat for youth, parents, and the youth ministry leadership to plan the year.
- Ask each parent to fill out or respond to a survey of what the year might bring.

Step 3. Inform parents throughout the year as youth ministry happens.
- Create a newsletter that announces and reports youth ministry activities.
- Send a personal letter outlining details and schedule.
- Ask for parental consent when necessary.
- Expect verbal youth reports.

INVOLVEMENT

Step 1. Invite the prayers of parents.
- Create a prayer calendar that includes the youth ministry calendar, birthdays, and important markers in the lives of youth like graduations, driver's licenses, and baptism.

- Include prayer reminders in the church bulletin and newsletter.
- Highlight the life and testimony of each youth at some point in the year.
- Pray for parents at youth group gatherings.

Step 2. Expect participation from parents.
- Ask each parent to sign up for involvement in at least one youth group activity.
- Include parent representatives on the youth ministry team.
- Invite parents to be guest resource persons.
- Sponsor a recreation night for youth and their parents.

> **"PARENTS** KNOW
> **THEIR KIDS BETTER**
> **THAN WE DO."**
>
> —Mike Yaconelli, "Syncho-Mesh Ministry: The Parent-Youth Worker Connection," *Youthworker*, 2:1, p. 21

Step 3. Ask for feedback from parents.
- Informally inquire of parents how they feel things are going.
- Ask parents to pay attention to youth reactions to youth group activities and keep a journal of their youth's spiritual growth.
- Invite letters and notes from parents to their youth to be given as words of encouragement and praise.
- Hold a midyear and year-end evaluation involving parents.

SENSITIVITY
Step 1. Recognize the parents' primary role.
- Show respect for family activities and schedules, assuring parents that youth don't have to be at everything.
- Prepare an information sheet on each parent or set of parents, noting phone numbers, emergency information, family physician, occupations, skills, and hobbies.
- Ask permission if you are uncertain about a youth group activity. Check to see if activities are consistent with the

parents' values and understanding of faithful discipleship.

- Invite youth to interview their parents on important issues.

Step 2. Provide resources to parents and families.

- Schedule occasional meetings for parents on adolescent development, needs, and issues.
- Avoid depending on parents for fund-raising efforts.
- Build a resource library for parents.
- Pray for the youth and their parents regularly.

Step 3. Honor the family.

- Highlight parents as role models and Christian witnesses.
- Provide ideas for celebrating birthdays and Mother's and Father's Day.
- Do a service project for each family in the youth group.
- Write thank-you notes, letters of appreciation, and affirmation postcards to parents.

WHAT IF THERE ARE NO PARENTS?

This is a fact of life for many teens, and volunteer youth sponsors need to be particularly attentive. Almost every one of the ideas above can be adapted for teens with guardians. When that is not an option, provide adult mentors for teens and include them in parent activities. A few more points:

- Use inclusive language. Don't always talk about moms and dads.
- Help all youth to become aware of the different kinds of families.
- Find out about the special rules and restrictions with which some youth without parents live.
- Be aware of the economic situation of youth without parents. Some youth group activities can be exclusive because of their cost.

Although Jesus called people to leave their fathers, forsake their families, and treat all Christians as brother and sisters, the Bible still affirms the family, however it is composed, as the primary social structure in the lives of children and youth. Youth ministry with the youth group should always support and affirm healthy families. With this attitude, parents become partners with youth sponsors and everyone—youth, parents, and sponsors—benefits.

CHAPTER 10
BOOST YOUR BATTERIES

Bruce and Denise were just about burnt out. Halfway into their third year as youth sponsors, they were beginning to dread every youth meeting and every youth event. Although they knew they were tired, they felt guilty and ashamed. They still loved the youth, but they were tired of dealing with immaturity. They still loved youth ministry, but they were frustrated by pranks and discipline problems. They were still committed to completing their terms, but they could hardly bear the thought of enduring the next year and a half.

Everyone who has ever been in youth ministry knows that it is one of the most physically, emotionally, and spiritually demanding tasks in the church. Planning for youth group meetings, preparing Bible studies, making travel arrangements, prodding youth leadership, eliciting parental support, and adjusting your own family life all take their toll on youth sponsors. Yet many sponsors love youth and ministry with youth. They never regret the time and energy they give. And they often won't say no when asked to continue for another term.

These youth sponsors are God's gift to youth and to the church, but all of us have those times when we need to rest and get our batteries recharged.

Battery boosters can take many forms. Sometimes we need a long charge, sometimes a quick charge. Sometimes the battery can get charged by being active and other times you just have to stop. There are even times when someone else needs to give you a jump start. Perhaps some of the following battery boosters will be just what you need to replenish your energy for ministry with youth:

1. Pray for your ministry. Ritch, a youth pastor, has a monthly discipline of attending a retreat center for an afternoon of prayer for the youth, youth sponsors, and youth ministry of his church. After his prayer retreat, Ritch returns with a load of ideas, clearer thoughts for improving youth ministry, and a new energy and excitement for ministry with youth. Although a full day may be difficult, many volunteer youth sponsors can set aside an hour alone or as a team for this kind of intense prayer. What is important is to take the time to pray for youth and your ministry with youth.

2. Read a good book. Too many youth sponsors read only program resources and rarely read books and articles that can teach about youth, their culture, and the nature of ministry with youth. Once or twice a year, read a book that stretches your thinking about ministry with youth. While you read, keep paper handy to record your thoughts. You will be amazed at the insights and ideas your reading will generate. In addition, subscribe (or ask your church to subscribe) to a youth ministry periodical.

3. Meet with others. Many youth sponsors feel like they are alone in their work when, in fact, they are not. All around them are others who are concerned and who are involved with youth. Teachers in the public school, Sunday school teachers, youth sponsors in other churches in the community, community social workers, and even parents are all people who might be willing to meet occasionally to discuss the issues, concerns, and demands of ministry with youth. Learn to create these opportunities. Sometimes you may have to take the initiative to create meetings. Other times you may have to take the time to attend meetings planned by others. However you do it, meeting with others engaged in youth ministry will encourage you, give you ideas, and take away feelings of isolation youth sponsors often have.

4. Train for youth ministry. From one day workshops, to weekend conferences, to week- or month-long courses, many national youth ministry organizations, local groups, and denominational offices plan youth ministry leadership training events. These events typically include mass sessions with energizing and motivational speakers, worship experiences that inspire and challenge, workshops on a host of issues, and conversations with others in ministry with youth. Attending these events generates new ideas and new networks of friendship with others in youth ministry. Congregations are often willing to help cover the costs for these events because they realize that everyone will benefit.

5. Take a vacation. If the whole youth ministry program is beginning to feel overwhelming, take a month off. Bruce and Denise were prime candidates for this battery-boosting strategy. To take a vacation from youth ministry, line up substitutes and make the necessary arrangements to be gone for a period of time to spend time alone or with family. If this idea creates anxiety, then it is likely exactly what is needed. Remember, ministry with youth is dependent on God.

> **"THE** SUPPLY
> ———
> **OF PASSION WITHIN**
> ———
> **THE INNER SPIRIT**
> ———
> **IS NOT INEXHAUSTIBLE."**
> ———
> —Tim Smith, 8 *Habits of an Effective Youth Worker*, p. 126

6. Invite some help. Too often youth sponsors feel they must do everything in youth ministry by themselves. Usually there are two reasons: either they are concerned that it won't be done well or they are afraid to ask for help. This is unfortunate because when a vacation from youth ministry is not possible, inviting others to help is the next best thing. So many people have so much to offer. People in the community and in the congregation have a wealth of life experience and spiritual insight that they are often willing to share with youth. Most of the time, they are just waiting to be asked.

If we want those who are most committed to ministering with youth to be able to continue their ministries for the long haul, we must be sensitive to their needs for rest and find ways to help them recharge their batteries. When we do this well, both they and our youth are the winners.

CHAPTER 11
UNCOVER YOUR RESOURCES

Mark and Jennifer were recently married, in their mid-twenties, energetic, inspired, and new youth sponsors. When the youth group met for the first planning meeting, Mark and Jennifer asked them, "What should we do this year?" After several minutes of silence, the youth group unanimously replied, "I don't know." Mark and Jennifer realized they needed help. In the following weeks they searched for resources that would help them in their youth ministry.

Most volunteer youth sponsors struggle to find program ideas and resources. They often know only one place to look, the local Christian bookstore. While most Christian bookstores carry a relatively small selection of youth ministry resources, a wealth of resources is available through various suppliers.

BOOKS

Begin building a youth ministry library, either personally or for your church library. Not only are you helping yourself, but you are helping those who will follow you. Ask pastors and others in youth ministry to recommend which books to get and which to avoid.

There are two major publishers of books for youth ministry:
1. Group Publishing, Inc., in Loveland, Colorado.
2. Youth Specialties, a division of Zondervan Publishing in Grand Rapids, Michigan.

Some of these publishers' books are better than others, but most are useful. Get their catalogs so you can either order direct or through your local bookstore.

Many denominations have publishing houses that produce

youth ministry resources. Check with yours and with others.

Classics and out-of-print youth ministry books can still be useful and can occasionally be found in used bookstores.

Other churches, conference resource libraries, and even public libraries may all have books on youth ministry that you can borrow.

MAGAZINES

Here is where you will find the most up-to-date ideas, research, and trends in youth ministry. Youth ministry magazines generally include quick programs, Bible studies, and other activities for those last-minute preparations.

Group magazine. This is probably the most useful magazine for volunteer youth sponsors. *Group* includes an even balance of research reports, program ideas, and leadership tips.

YouthWorker Journal. This quarterly journal is geared for the youth pastor or the pastor with youth ministry responsibilities. It offers few program resources, but includes many thought-provoking articles on theology, philosophy, and administration of youth ministry. It will be useful to the volunteer youth sponsor who wants to dig deeper into youth ministry.

Several other magazines and journals provide some useful information and ideas, but may not be worth a subscription: *Campus Life: Leader's Edition*, *Religious Education*, and *Christian Education*.

Some denominational publishing houses publish youth ministry magazines or journals for youth sponsors. While these reflect their denominational connections, many of these are as good as, if not better than, more well-known publications. Examples include: *YouthGuide* from Faith & Life Press.

Magazines that address social and theological issues can provide invaluable resources, especially for teaching. Examples include: *Sojourners*, *Christianity Today*, *Christian Century*, and *Media and Values*.

Finally, don't dismiss the popular magazines and newspapers. *Time*, *Newsweek*, *McLeans*, *Rolling Stone*, *Seventeen*, *People*, and many others include articles that address teen issues, teen trends, and teen experiences.

ELECTRONIC MEDIA

Videos and music are an important part of youth ministry. Although you must avoid creating a video-based youth ministry, you also should not be afraid to use video and music resources with youth. They are, after all, a significant element in the lives of most youth. Group Publishing and Youth Specialties, as well as some denominational publishers, produce video resources. Most can be borrowed from Christian bookstores, denominational resource libraries, and video stores.

PEOPLE

People make issues and ideas come alive. Every volunteer youth sponsor has access to hundreds of people who can contribute to the youth ministry program. Most people are reasonably expert in at least one or two areas. The key is taking the risk to invite them.

First, develop a list of potential people you want to ask. Then, make two columns on a piece of paper and write the names of those who consent in the first column. In the second, write their areas of interest. In the margin, keep track of when they help. Continually add to the list. The following categories of people may help you get started:

- your pastor and other pastors;
- parents;
- denominational staff;
- youth and young adults;
- missionaries and service workers;
- international students;
- people of specific occupations: physicians, teachers, farmers, social workers, journalists, etc.

PLACES

Sometimes the most significant youth group experiences happen in settings other than the local church. One youth minister received permission to hold a Bible study on Philippians in a local jail cell. Other possibilities include:

- cemetery,

- zoo,
- workplace,
- camp,
- museum or gallery,
- park,
- YMCA/recreation center,
- campus,
- out-of-doors,
- warehouse.

EVENTS

Two types of events can be useful for youth ministry: events intended for youth, and events intended for youth sponsors:

1. Many youth groups have gone to a concert together, but other events may be more meaningful, challenging, and inspiring. These include:

- peer baptisms or confirmations,
- dramas,
- worship services of other denominations or religions,
- political rallies,
- lectures,
- camps, conferences, and other churchwide events.

2. Among the most underused resources for sponsors are training events. Many of these events happen year-round and offer excellent opportunities for learning and inspiration. Consider the following:

- Youth Specialties and Group offer youth ministry training opportunities year-round all over North America. If you are on their mailing lists, you will hear about them.
- Many public school districts offer teacher in-service training. These are often highly motivational and informative. Check with your local principal about attending.
- Social workers and health care professionals also attend in-service events, some of which address adolescent issues. Rubbing shoulders with people working outside the church who care about youth can also be very enlightening.

- Denominations often offer youth ministry training events. These are usually of excellent quality and reasonably priced.

ODDS & ENDS

One whole group of resources most people never consider is the simple stuff that is a part of everyday life. Imagining how your youth might use everyday stuff can be almost as much fun as watching them use it.

- Colored pens and pencils. Why write in black and white? The world is much more colorful.
- Colored gum balls, balloons, candy, and rubber bands offer creative ways to form small groups.
- Paintings and photographs can be great discussion starters.

> **"THERE'S** A LOT
>
> **MORE CREATIVE**
>
> **STUFF HIDING OUT THERE**
>
> **THAN THERE USED TO BE."**
>
> —Tim McLughlin, *Youthworker*, 11:3, p. 1

- Pipe cleaners and modeling clay invite creative expression of motions.
- And the list could go on and on…

Jesus used the stuff of life to create parables to teach about God's love and God's kingdom. Still, the most important resource was Jesus himself. In the same way, you are the most important ministry resource. A caring, compassionate, listening, testifying, adult is more important than all the resources money can buy, because you are God's living word to youth.

PART 2

WOR-
SHIP

CHAPTER 12
INVITE FAITH IN CHRIST

It was one of those glorious moments in youth ministry. Jeff approached Alan, his youth sponsor, and said he wanted to become a Christian. Alan's eyes lit up, he and Jeff found a quiet place to pray, and Jeff made the commitment that changed his life.

Inviting youth to faith in Jesus Christ is the first goal of youth ministry. It grows out of Jesus' great commission to all his disciples to preach the gospel. Thus, it is something every volunteer youth sponsor needs to be able to do.

When young people enter adolescence, they begin a new journey of discovery about what life means, what is important, what to believe in, and what to commit to. For some it is an easy journey; for others, a difficult one. Some begin with many advantages—a Christian family, a childhood in the church, a Christian school, or a sense of God's presence in their lives. Others have few or no advantages. They may have never been in a church. They may not know Christmas is the celebration of Jesus' birth. They may only know God's name as an expletive. Yet, both groups of youth and those many in-between often find solidarity with one another in their common faith questions. It is a rare young person who does not wonder about the existence of God, the problem of evil, life after death, and the wonder of God's love.

> ## "TO OFFER
> ## GOOD NEWS, WE
> ## MUST BE GOOD NEWS."
>
> —Jeff Johnson, *Evangelization*, p. 60

One of the greatest joys of youth ministry is to walk with young people as they travel this road, ask their questions, and discover their own faith. When struggling with their faith questions, many youth turn to significant adults in their lives for different perspectives and guidance. Youth sponsors are in a tremendous position to be available to youth and to invite them to consider following Jesus Christ. The key is to be prepared for the opportunities when they arise.

The New Testament offers several examples of how to invite people to faith. The Emmaus story in Luke 24 portrays Jesus modeling a relational approach to sharing faith. Paul's preaching ministry in Acts offers a more explicit invitational approach. Peter and Stephen, although they preached the gospel, often got into trouble for sharing their faith through example, for doing the work of Christ. With young people, all of these approaches can work, especially if the basic principles are combined and become a part of the youth group experience.

PRINCIPLE 1: BE READY TO TELL YOUR OWN FAITH STORY.

Periodically write out your faith story, recounting those moments when God touched your life and brought you close. As you write, you define your story more clearly. You begin to choose and emphasize the conversion points when you made changes towards God. In writing your faith story, you can see the places where your story may sound familiar to a young person struggling with a similar issue or faith question.

PRINCIPLE 2: WALK WITH YOUTH.

The opportunity to invite youth to faith in Christ comes only when you are with them. Youth sponsors need to be on the turf of young people, see their struggles, hear their cries of sorrow and joy, and empathize with the realities in their lives. This gives you integrity with youth so that they will trust you with their deepest needs, fears, and hopes.

PRINCIPLE 3: HEAR AND INVITE YOUNG PEOPLE'S QUESTIONS.

Presence with youth provides both the opportunity to hear what they are talking about and to enter into the conversation by

Quick Tip
FIVE WAYS TO INVITE FAITH QUESTIONS

1. Ask youth to bring a song that raises their faith question.
2. Place a question box in the youth room.
3. Have a group journal for three or four months and invite youth to write in it whenever they wish.
4. Challenge youth to mold a lump of clay into something that represents their faith question.
5. Ask each youth to write a faith question on a small piece of paper, place it in a balloon, blow it up, pin it to a bulletin board, and throw a dart to choose the faith question of the week.

raising questions and issues with them. Too often adults don't listen to youth, yet expect youth to listen to them. Only when youth believe adults are listening are they able to listen to adults.

PRINCIPLE 4: OFFER YOUR FAITH STORY AS A POINT OF VIEW.

Like it or not, you cannot turn a young person into a Christian. You can tell your story, share your perspective, and answer questions with the answers you have discovered. Youth may listen. Youth may agree. But, they may reject your point of view. That is their prerogative. So, offer your story as *your* perspective and it will probably be received better than if you offer it as *the* perspective.

PRINCIPLE 5: PRAY WITH YOUTH AND EMBRACE THEIR STEPS.

Most people understand coming to faith in Jesus Christ as a journey, a series of steps taken throughout life. This is as true for youth as it is for adults. Youth often need others to walk with them as they take steps toward faith in Christ. Youth sponsors can hold their hands, pray with them, hear their confessions, and celebrate their commitments. With youth, formulas are less important than the person who prays beside them. And in God's ears, the cry for mercy, forgiveness, and love always has integrity, regardless of the words used.

Every young person must claim a personal faith in Jesus Christ in his or her own time. Youth sponsors simply tell the story, listen to the questions, and celebrate the commitments. When it happens, it is one of the most glorious moments in youth ministry!

CHAPTER 13
DISCIPLE FAITH
IN CHRIST

It happened over and over again. Every time Esther went to camp or a youth event, she always heard the speaker give an invitation to either accept Christ or rededicate her life to Christ. Because the message always made Esther doubt her faith, she was scared into rededicating her life to Christ repeatedly. No one ever told Esther that what she needed was to be discipled.

Evangelism assumes that a person is not a Christian; *discipleship* assumes that a person is a Christian. As a starting point, these are helpful distinctions. But disciples—Christians—still need to hear good news because we all fail and we are never fully converted. The speakers at Esther's youth events overlooked these distinctions. They ignored the fact that some youth were Christians. They assumed that most were unconverted and the rest were backslidden Christians who needed to be converted again. Esther and her friends knew they were both Christians *and* sinners. What they needed was to be discipled.

Some youth are not yet Christians and some youth are Christians. Ministry to the first group is a ministry of inviting youth to faith in Jesus Christ. It is the ministry of evangelism. Ministry to the second group is a ministry of inviting youth to follow Jesus Christ. It is the ministry of discipling.

Discipling invites youth to follow Jesus with increasingly greater steps of obedience and deeper friendship with God—*worship*. Discipling teaches youth about the responsibilities of life in the kingdom with the brothers and sisters of faith—*community*. Discipling calls youth to involvement in mission and service, touching the life of the world with the word-and-deed good news of Jesus Christ—*mission*. In ongoing ways, a disciple of Jesus Christ might be engaged in these three areas through:

Worship
- Bible study,
- corporate worship,
- prayer.

Community
- teaching Sunday school,
- listening to a friend's problem,
- giving an offering.

Mission
- personal evangelism,
- aiding in a disaster,
- working with the homeless.

The youth group is a setting for discipling. The quality of a young person's discipling experience may be related to how intentional youth sponsors are in defining the youth group as a discipling setting. Other discipling settings in the congregation might include Sunday school, catechism, and the family.

If we use Jesus and his disciples as our example, we will recognize several steps in the discipling process that can apply to the youth group:

1. The call. Youth must continually be called to deeper and more extensive commitments to follow Jesus Christ. These calls will honor the initial decision to become a Christian and they will help youth to understand the Christian faith as a journey. Youth can then be called to take further steps along the way. These steps might include a commitment to put others first, saying yes to a call to a specific ministry, or starting a spiritual discipline of journaling.

"REAL-LIFE

DISCIPLESHIP IS WHAT

HAPPENS BETWEEN THE MEETINGS."

—Duffy Robbins, *The Ministry of Nurture*, p. 55

2. The teaching. Youth must be taught the story of God, the good news of Jesus Christ, and the history of God's people. For the disciple, a certain amount of knowledge is basic. Jesus, in teaching his disciples, built upon the foundations of their religious education. Youth, as well, still need much of that basic teaching so they can discover how God has worked and continues to work in the world. Learning God's story in the Bible, the early church, the denomination, or the contemporary world helps youth imagine the ways God may work in their lives and in the world they touch.

3. The model. Youth must see in youth sponsors a model of a disciple of Jesus Christ. In spite of all Jesus taught his disciples, it was his life that finally convinced them of the good news because his life gave flesh to his teachings. Youth sponsors, as well as other adults in the church, are the flesh of Jesus to youth. Through you, youth discover the meaning of grace, forgiveness, joy, and life. Therefore, you must examine your spiritual life, your social life, your family life, and your vocational life, making sure you are following Jesus as best you can in every way.

4. The act. Youth must be engaged in acts of discipleship. Jesus' disciples discovered the power of forgiveness, healing, liberation, and salvation as they watched it happen in the

Quick Tip
WHAT IF THE YOUTH IN OUR GROUP ARE NOT ALL CHRISTIANS

Option 1: Treat the youth group as a discipling setting, inviting youth who are not yet Christians to observe and learn what it "costs" to be Christian.

Option 2: Create a special setting for discipling youth. Mentoring, pairing a new Christian with an older Christian, is one excellent setting for discipling. A discipleship group is another. If you form a discipleship group, the youth group then becomes a setting primarily for evangelism or fellowship.

Option 3: Plan special outreach events to provide opportunities for inviting youth to faith in Christ. Then the youth group can become the discipling setting where these youth are taught the way of Jesus Christ.

lives of others. The same is true for youth today. The power of sacrifice and love are best learned through touching the lives of others. Encourage youth to tell the story of their faith to their friends. Encourage youth to serve the church with their gifts. Encourage youth to debate the issues of faith and faithfulness. Encourage youth to get into the world and serve others in the name of Christ. These acts themselves will help youth grow as disciples.

The responsibility for discipling is both theirs and ours. Youth can and should take responsibility for their lives as followers of Jesus Christ. Without some self-motivation, there is little we can do. At the same time, we also have responsibility for helping to grow the faith of youth. Jesus anguished many times over the hardness and failures of his disciples. Yet, he continued to call, teach, model, and invite his disciples into his ministry. Above all, we must remember that God's Spirit is also involved, guiding youth sponsors and youth to discover the good news of Jesus Christ.

CHAPTER 14
MENTOR THE SPIRITUAL LIFE

After spending a full day on the road and stuffing donuts in their mouths, Wendell and his youth group piled into the car for another full day of driving. After a few minutes, Wendell turned to his right and saw Cristie pull out her Bible, a devotional book, and her journal and begin her morning devotions. In spite of a late night of pizza, TV, and goofing around; in spite of raucous conversation in the back seat; in spite of Led Zeppelin blaring on the stereo; Cristie disciplined herself to cultivate her spiritual life. Wendell sat at the steering wheel in awe.

It is amazing to discover the depth of the spiritual life of some young people. Though many youth keep a schedule that would drive most adults insane, it is always a delight to find yet another young person who has cultivated one of the disciplines of the spiritual life. It is encouraging and reassuring to find youth interested in "learning to become God's friend," Richard Foster's definition for spirituality.

As one aspect of discipleship, cultivating the disciplines of the spiritual life is more intentionally focused on the inner life, the devotional life. It is a way to communicate with God. It is a way to enter into the presence of God. It is a way to grow in friendship with God. It is a way to follow Jesus into the wilderness to meet God, discover God's will, and be empowered by God's Spirit.

Like Cristie, some youth nurture their inner spiritual lives by practicing morning devotions, daily Bible reading, and prayer. These highly self-motivated youth are reaping the rewards of friendship with God. But many youth who want a deeper relationship with God through the spiritual disciplines are not able to keep at it on their own. They are like the disciples who were easily distracted and misunderstood the purpose of Jesus' quiet times in the wilderness. These youth may need to be given the tools of spiritual discipline. They may need to be mentored in the use of these tools. And they may need a support group to help them use the tools until they become second nature. The youth group can be a setting where the spiritual life can be cultivated.

Richard Foster, in *Celebration of Discipline*, identifies twelve spiritual disciplines under three headings. Each of these can be practiced through the youth group with varying levels of involvement for the whole group. In the most involved way, the youth group can become a community of discipline with every person participating in one or more spiritual disciplines and sharing their progress at each meeting with the group. In a less involved way, the youth group can offer a setting for experimenting. Different disciplines are tried briefly by the whole group. Then individual youth are invited to go on from there. In the least involved way, the youth group can be the setting where the different spiritual disciplines are taught and discussed. Each youth in the group is then invited to begin practicing one or more disciplines individually.

"THE SPIRITUAL LIFE IS AS MUCH CAUGHT AS TAUGHT."

If you do decide to begin working at the spiritual disciplines, remember the following principles: First, high school youth are still young. They may not fully understand the meaning of the disciplines nor be able to plow deeply in them. Beginning is often the most successful act. Second, set small goals. It may be best to practice one discipline, four days a week, for a month. Finally, provide ways for youth to share their progress. A graffiti wall, sharing times, a public youth group journal, or private meetings with youth sponsors all provide youth with opportunities to share the joys and successes of spiritual life.

THE INWARD DISCIPLINES

1. Meditation invites youth to times of silence to listen for God. Using a devotional book is a common way young people meditate. Other possibilities include:
- reflecting on God's creative power out-of-doors,
- memorizing a Scripture passage,
- writing in a journal.

2. Prayer is conversation with God. For many youth, prayer is a mealtime or bedtime activity, but Colossians invites us to pray without ceasing so that God is our ever-present friend. Practicing the discipline of prayer can include:
- everyone in the group agreeing to pray at noon,
- writing a group prayer that everyone memorizes and recites daily,
- soliciting prayer requests or using a directory as a prayer resource.

3. Fasting is a rarely practiced, though commonly known, spiritual discipline that usually involves not eating for a period of time so that hunger for food becomes a reminder to hunger for God. For health reasons, active growing youth should use this discipline with great care, but food is not the only thing from which to fast. Youth might fast by:
- not driving but depending on others for transportation,
- replacing TV, movies, or music with Bible reading, service, or prayer,
- giving an equivalent amount for each fast-food meal to relieve world hunger.

4. Study is the intentional effort to discover God and the way God works through careful reading, thoughtful contemplation, and energetic discussion of Scripture and other writings of the church. Most youth know study as a school experience, but few know study as a spiritual experience. Youth can be invited into the discipline of study through:
- memorizing long passages of Scripture, such as the Sermon on the Mount,
- a study retreat focusing on a book of the Bible or a short classic from Christian history,

- celebrating and taking more seriously the Bible study or Sunday school hour as a spiritual discipline.

THE OUTWARD DISCIPLINES

5. Simplicity invites youth to rid themselves of the trappings of consumerism. There are many challenging ways to invite youth to simplicity:

- let go of one involvement that makes life too busy,
- wear only non-name-brand and non-advertised clothing for a month,
- get permission to go without shoes for a week.

6. Solitude is time intentionally spent alone in the presence of God. It can provide youth with the chance to discover the joy of being alone without feeling lonely. Solitude can be practiced by:

- not talking for an entire day at a camp or a retreat,
- creating a "place for solitude" in the youth room,
- noticing the moments of solitude in everyday life and cherishing them as opportunities to be with God.

7. Submission requires letting go of the need to have things done "my" way. It lifts others up, invites others forward, and, in Jesus' words, "denies self" to follow Christ. Although submission may be one of the most difficult disciplines for youth in our society, it is one of the most needed. Youth can discover submission through:

- letting go of offensive or demeaning language,
- giving special privileges to someone else,
- making a commitment to follow the wishes of others for a period of time.

8. Service is a spiritual discipline that many youth experience but rarely understand as an element of the spiritual life. Helping youth to see service as a spiritual discipline can give it new meaning. This can be accomplished by:

- keeping a journal during service experiences,
- committing to service on a regular basis,
- beginning a friendship with a person on the fringe.

THE CORPORATE DISCIPLINES

9. Confession is the invitation to lay before God and others
our sins and our failures. Since we live in a time when denial of
wrongdoing is common, it is important to invite youth to learn
the freedom that lies in the expression of confession and the
experience of forgiveness. Youth can be invited to:

- own up to the times when they deny their immorality,
- keep an anonymous confessional journal where messages
  and prayers of forgiveness can be given,
- welcome youth who take the risk to share their sins.

10. Worship is when we give our attention to the glory of
God and God's mighty acts of salvation and love on our behalf.
Most youth groups experience worship with the congregation,
but worship can also be experienced through the youth group by:

- creating services of worship for occasional youth group
  gatherings,
- praying for those preparing and leading worship with the
  congregation,
- writing worship materials that speak to the needs and
  interests of youth.

**11. Guidance comes through seeking to know God's will
for life.** This is often one of the chief concerns of young people.
Youth can enter into the discipline of guidance through:

- sharing coming decisions with the youth group for their
  counsel,
- making commitments to follow through on what they
  already know to do,
- studying the decisions that the church has wrestled with
  on issues of belief and Christian practice.

12. Celebration is the ability to party because of what God
has done and is doing in our lives. Youth often rightly critique
their congregations for their inability, even refusal, to celebrate.
The youth group can experience celebration by:

- throwing parties for the church,
- creating celebrations for significant moments in life such
  as graduations, driving licenses, and new steps of faithfulness,

- planning a comedy night so laughter can be the healing force that God created it to be.

Inviting youth to cultivate the spiritual life may be one of the most important things youth sponsors and youth groups can do. For many youth, it may be the only place they ever hear about developing a deep friendship with God. Most youth carry a longing in their hearts for cultivating the spiritual life. Our opportunity is to provide the tools.

CHAPTER 15
PRACTICE PRAYER

There it was again—dead silence. Reed and Susan had tried over and over to involve their youth group in prayer, and nearly every time—dead silence.

Practicing prayer in the youth group setting can be one of the most rewarding or one of the most frustrating experiences in youth ministry. The old adage "you've got to work with what you get" is never more true than with prayer in the youth group setting. Prayer within the youth group is clearly related to prayer in the everyday lives of your youth. When prayer is a part of their lives, it will more easily be a part of youth group life. If youth are not praying outside the youth group, they are not likely to pray within the youth group unless you take the initiative to help your youth group learn to practice prayer.

> ## "CONTINUE
> ### IN PRAYER
> ### ALWAYS."
>
> —Paul, 1 Thessalonians 5:17

STEP 1: DECIDE TO PRAY.

Make the decision to include prayer in every youth group experience. Pray before eating snacks. Pray before driving to the bowling alley. Pray for the youth who failed to come. Pray for the family who just experienced a funeral. When prayer becomes a common experience for the youth group, youth begin to feel more at ease and accept the place of prayer in their gatherings. Then youth discover that it is okay to pray at any time for anything.

STEP 2: START SMALL.

Begin with periods of silent prayer. Silent prayer is an opportunity to pray for things that cannot be spoken. Confession, prayers for secret concerns, and pleas for hope and deliverance are often best offered in silence. Help youth to understand that not everything needs to be spoken aloud, that prayer whispered in the quiet is just as legitimate as public prayer. When praying in silence, pay attention to time. Too often five minutes of silence is cut short after thirty seconds because we are not used to the slower pace of silence.

After a few periods of silent prayer, try sentence prayers. First, spend five minutes brainstorming a list of prayer concerns. Then, invite each youth to offer a sentence prayer, choosing an item from the prayer concern list. If someone chooses not to participate, that's okay, but encourage them to try next time. It will take time for some youth to feel comfortable baring their souls publicly before God and their peers. Eventually, as youth feel more comfortable with sentence prayers, they will begin to lengthen their prayers. Soon they will be ready to lead prayer in the youth group and other public settings.

STEP 3: PRACTICE PRAYER.

Remind yourself and teach youth that prayer requires practice. Even Jesus had to teach the disciples how to pray. Remembering this can be reassuring as you begin incorporating prayer into the youth group experience. Knowing this will also help youth gain confidence as they begin to practice prayer in the youth group.

STEP 4: USE A PRAYER KEY.

Prayer keys help you learn about and practice prayer. The following are three examples.

Key 1—ACTS

A doration—statements that reflect the greatness of God.

C onfession—admissions of sin and failure, or statements of faith and belief.

T hanksgiving—expressions of gratitude for the needs and blessings of life.

S upplication—requests for personal needs or the needs of others.

Key 2—The Lord's Prayer, Matthew 6:9-13

1. Words of praise and honor to God.
2. Invitation for the coming of the kingdom.
3. Affirmations of God's will.
4. Request for everyday needs.
5. Request for forgiveness of sin.
6. Request for strength against evil.

Key 3—The Mission Prayer, Acts 1:8

1. Jerusalem—prayer for the city.
2. Judea—prayer for the state or province.
3. Samaria—prayer for the country.
4. Ends of the earth—prayer for the world.

STEP 5: MAKE PRAYER REAL.

Ask youth to pray about real issues that need their prayers. Too often youth don't know what to pray for, so they pray in general terms. When doing this, youth can easily become discouraged because the issues loom large and it is difficult to see how change can be effected, especially by "just" prayer. Therefore, encourage youth to be specific in relation to person, place, and time. And, sometimes, pray for a specific thing for a specified period of time. It is sometimes helpful to use a news magazine or newspaper as a source for prayer concerns.

Prayer is the most powerful force on earth. It recognizes God's control over all things, and it celebrates and expects God's involvement in our lives. Above all, prayer helps youth understand that God walks with them through their lives, helping them to carry the weight of the many changes and decisions they daily face.

CHAPTER 16
DIG INTO BIBLE STUDY

Of all the youth ministry settings in the church, Corey's Wednesday evening Bible studies with the youth group were the best attended and the most highly rated. Youth brought their friends, and their friends kept coming back. As word spread, people began to wonder what Corey's secret was.

Almost every person in youth ministry has wondered, How do you get youth excited about Bible study? There are no magic answers. Corey, in fact, didn't have any secrets; he just did hard work. He began with the belief that Bible study was important, it should be well done, and he could do it. Corey then practiced five basic principles for teaching and learning.

PRINCIPLE 1: PLAN.

More important than curriculum, more important than creativity, more important than technique, planning is the first ingredient to successful learning experiences. Make an appointment with yourself to sit down and prepare whether you are using a curriculum or not.

> **"THE** BEST
>
> **WAY TO TEACH THE**
>
> **BIBLE IS THROUGH ACTIONS."**
>
> —M. Scott Peck, as quoted by Bill McNabb and Steven Mabry in *Teaching the Bible Creatively*, p. 11

PRINCIPLE 2: PRAY.

When you teach, you never teach alone. Invite the Holy Spirit to plan, study, design, and teach with you.

Quick Tip
CURRICULUM?

Using a curriculum is neither good nor bad. Keep in mind the following when choosing whether or not to use a curriculum:

1. Creating your own curriculum takes a lot of time to do well, but using a curriculum well also involves time. Planning is important to both.

2. You never have to use a curriculum as it is. Always adapt it to your situation and the needs of your youth. This will also help you gain skill in writing your own curriculum.

3. Pay attention to who wrote and who published the curriculum. Curriculum writers and publishers bring a theological bias to the Bible and faith issues just as you do. Knowing their perspective allows you to affirm or reject the bias.

Finally, don't be afraid to create your own curriculum. Following the plan outlined in this chapter will make it a much easier task than you might imagine. After all, much of what you can buy was originally created by folks just like you!

PRINCIPLE 3: STUDY.

At least a week ahead, review the material you plan to teach. If you are using a curriculum, this is easy; just sit down and read through the lesson. If you are not using a curriculum, choose a topic and begin your research. Books, magazine articles, and people are your resources. As you read and learn, make notes of any ideas you have for the lesson you intend to teach.

PRINCIPLE 4: DESIGN.

On a blank paper, design your lesson plan. First, write the Scripture text or topic at the top of the page. Second, identify one or two goals for the learning experience. Third, choose and create the learning experiences you will use and note the resources you will need. Every learning experience should include five elements:

1. **Focus** attention to the issue. This activity seeks to excite interest in the issue. It responds to a young person's need to have a reason to pay attention.

2. **Connect** the issue to the life experience of youth. This element responds to the need for relevance.

3. **Dig** into the issue by studying the Scripture text and the other resources the teacher has discovered. Although this is often the information-giving

element, it should rarely be a lecture. Youth are quite capable of discovering the necessary information themselves.

4. **Re-connect** the issue back to the life of youth. Often called application, this activity also addresses relevancy, but with the new information from the previous activity.

5. **Respond** by inviting youth to actively make a decision to do something about what they have learned. This necessary element makes what has been learned real and helps youth discover that Bible study can be life-changing.

In designing your lesson plan, think creatively. Youth learn best through active learning experiences, so each element in the lesson plan should involve at least two of the senses. Creativity is not a gift; it is a learned way of thinking that must be practiced.

PRINCIPLE 5: PLAN AGAIN.

Once the lesson is designed, list the materials you will need and gather them. Then walk through the lesson to make sure you will meet your intended goals. During this step, don't hesitate to re-create your learning activities if new ideas come. At the same time, remember that you must, at some point, go with your plan.

Whether it is a Wednesday evening Bible study, a Sunday school class, or some other learning setting, when the hour comes, gather up your confidence, walk into the room, and enter into the Bible study experience. More often than not, it will go well. If it doesn't, keep at it; youth may not be used to a creative teacher and an exciting Bible study experience!

Here are ten activities that can be transformed into creative Bible study experiences:

1. **Video interviews** inviting one- or two-minute answers to "What do you think...?"

2. **3- to 5-minute excerpts from TV or films** asking how the issue is addressed or what the characters might think.

3. **Objects and stuff** which visually illustrate the text or the topic. Can you represent the nouns in the text?

4. **Stories** that connect the text or the issue to someone's real life can be read, told, or watched.

5. **Excursions** into the real world where youth live, study, play, and work. Most of the biblical story happened out-of-doors.

6. **Music** can be used to raise the issue, create a discussion, or invite worship.

7. **Food** may not be related to the lesson, but it can often help the learning! Maybe that's why Jesus' followers worshiped, studied, and ate together.

8. **Actions** can help youth mimic the text or topic and bring it home.

9. **Projects,** such as skits, dramas, readings, sculptures, art, service acts, performances, etc., can be both creative learning experiences and meaningful final products.

10. **Role plays** allow youth to emotionally sympathize with the text or the topic.

YOUTH GROUP
BIBLE STUDY PLANNING WORKSHEET

Lesson Title: _____

Date: _____

Scripture: _____

Goals:

    • _____

    • _____

	EXPERIENCE	RESOURCES
Focus • attention to the issue. • Are you interested?		
Connect • the issue to life. • How is this issue relevant?		
Dig • into the Scripture. • How was it/is it understood.		
Re-Connect • the issue back to life. • What is the story's relevance?		
Respond • by doing something about what was learned.		

CHAPTER 17
HANDLE HOT TOPICS

Mike knew there would be no way around it. With the encouragement of youth and parents, he agreed to begin a study on sexuality with the youth group. He knew their study would bring up the issue of abortion just as inevitably as it would bring up the question "So how far can we go?" How could he handle this explosive topic in a way that was sensitive to the questions and concerns of the youth, faithful to biblical teaching, and consistent with the position of his church?

Most youth sponsors will occasionally need to address hot topics. As youth discover the world around them, meet new people, and hear different ideas, the hot topics of the day will raise questions for them. When these topics come up, the worst thing a youth sponsor can do is ignore them or shrug them off. When this happens, many youth take it as a sign that either the church has nothing to say or that the church doesn't trust them to grapple with the topic. Either way, youth get a negative message, and the church is shirking its task of discipling youth in Christian faith. It is critical, therefore, for youth sponsors to either be prepared or take time to become prepared when these topics come up.

Hot topics are important because they are real! When youth raise an issue, it is often because they have personally encountered it in some way. The youth in Mike's group knew youth who had had abortions. They knew there were different viewpoints in their community and in their church. And they knew they might face the issue personally. Because it was a live issue for them, they brought the topic to the church, and to Mike, for guidance.

In response, Mike and his church took the following steps to address this and other hot topics.

STEP 1: INFORM ALL CONCERNED PERSONS THAT THE TOPIC HAS BEEN RAISED AND YOU INTEND TO STUDY IT WITH THE YOUTH GROUP.

If more people are in the know, fewer people will choose to criticize. This means, at the very least, that parents should be informed when hot topics will be studied. Enlisting the support and counsel of the pastor and other church leadership may also be an advantage.

STEP 2: PREPARE, PLAN, AND PRAY.

Hot topics cannot be handled lightly or carelessly. Read some current books and magazine and journal articles on the topic. If it is useful, choose a curriculum to help you teach the topic. Enlist the aid of experts. Find out what resources and official statements your denomination has published on the topic. Plan your study carefully by deciding the number of sessions and the theme for each session. Pray throughout the entire process for the leading and guidance of God's Spirit.

> **Possible Hot Topics**
> - What God?
> - Sex—what's God got to do with it?
> - Why did God make AIDS?
> - My friend's name is Muhammad.
> - Hell? No.
> - Gay used to mean happy.
> - The Bible, believe it or not?
> - Cussing, swearing, and other naughty words.
> - *War & Peace* by men and their toys.
> - Get a life. Why?

STEP 3: WHENEVER POSSIBLE, USE THE BIBLICAL STORY AS A STORY RATHER THAN AS A PROOF TEXT.

Most hot topics are related to human experience, and most human experiences are addressed in biblical stories. The biblical stories allow youth to think about how they might have reacted. They can discover how God and God's people addressed the topic. Finally, they can interpret their own experiences and possible responses in the light of God's Word on the topic. Proof texting is much easier to accept *and* reject without thinking. Stories stretch the mind.

STEP 4: RECOGNIZE THAT YOUTH ARE ON A JOURNEY OF LIFE AND FAITH DISCOVERY.

They may not be looking for answers on a topic. They may just want information or an opinion to weigh against others they are hearing. If you are unsure about a topic, it is okay to admit your uncertainty. Don't offer pat answers to difficult issues. Youth are discovering that the world is grey. Black and white answers to grey issues don't ring true. Youth don't expect adults to have everything figured out, but they do expect adults to be honest.

STEP 5: REMEMBER THAT YOUTH ARE MORE LIKELY TO HOLD A POSITION THEY HAVE DISCOVERED THAN ONE THEY HAVE BEEN TOLD.

Youth can be given the freedom to grapple with hot topics. They are beginning to think critically about the world and the church. When given the opportunity and good information, youth often respect their Christian faith and choose positions consistent with their understanding of God. When they disagree with an orthodox opinion, relax; they are likely to rethink the topic later, anyway. Sometimes youth sponsors must remember that God gives the freedom to choose what to believe to youth as well as adults.

In Mike's youth group, the study went as he expected. Abortion came up. He shared the church's perspective. They looked at the biblical stories. They listened to current thinking. There

"DIALOG

IS IMPORTANT."

—Tony Campolo, *20 Hot Potatoes Christians Are Afraid to Touch*, p. 235

was a lot of discussion, and most of the youth chose not to take a strong position. For many of them, it wasn't even an issue; they were just curious. Likely that topic will confront them again. When it does, they will have a foundation of what they have learned within the context of the faith community to build upon.

CHAPTER 18
MAKE MUSIC

Maria doesn't play guitar or piano, and she can't sight-read a song. Although she sings in the church choir, Maria would never sing a solo, and she learns her part by listening to the altos around her. Maria has no background or education in music, but she knows music and singing are important. In fact, Maria loves music and singing. And Maria, a passionate youth sponsor as well as a lover of music, believes music should be a part of the worship experience of her youth group.

Probably no other force moves people like music. Every culture in every time has made music part of their worship, their oral history, and their important celebrations. Music can speak to the heart. It can record the stories of a

> **"MUSIC IS WORSHIP WHEN IT BECOMES AN EXPRESSION OF FAITH."**
>
> —Thomas N. Tomaszek, *Liturgy and Worship*, p. 86

people. It can celebrate the joy and pleasure of life. It is the one aspect of art and culture in which every person participates, either as creator or listener.

Music is and should be a key ingredient in the worship life of the youth group. Traditionally, youth groups sing choruses, gospel songs, or hymns accompanied by guitar or piano. In years past, youth hymnals and songbooks were common in many churches. Today, however, many youth groups struggle to include music. Fewer youth play guitar, the standard accompaniment for youth songs. Youth are passive consumers of music more often than its creators or performers. Yet, whether youth are creators or listeners, music can be an important part of the youth group worship experience.

LISTENING TO MUSIC AS WORSHIP.

Many youth group sponsors roll their eyes when they try to lead singing and half the group, often the guys, sit slouched in their chairs with teeth clenched and lips tight. The assumption—everyone will sing; the reality—some just won't! This does not mean, however, that those who are not singing do not appreciate the experience. What they probably don't like is the expectation that they sing. For them, listening to the song can be just as important as singing it.

How can listening to music be a worship experience?

1. Listening to others sing. This often happens anyway, but it can be done more intentionally.

- Invite an ensemble, quartet, or trio to bring a song.
- When singing together, use an old songleader's technique—invite guys to sing one verse, girls another.
- Sing antiphonally.
- Encourage humming or other kinds of voice instrumentation.

2. Listening to recorded music.

- Songs related to the theme for the evening can be played as youth are entering the meeting room.
- Listening to a song and reading its lyrics can be incorporated into the study or worship experience.
- Recorded music can be played and youth invited to sing along.

3. Listening to the songs. Listening is not just the act of hearing. It includes paying attention to what is heard.

- Study the theology of a song by using it as a text. What does the song say about God, about following Jesus, and about others?
- Study the lyrics of a song to discover what message the song writer is trying to communicate.
- Study the history or story of a song. Hymnal handbooks tell the often turbulent stories of familiar hymns and songs.
- Memorize lyrics as a poem, not a song. This can open new insights into a song's message.

CREATING MUSIC AS A WORSHIP EXPERIENCE.

Whether through composition or performance, creating music reaches into the soul, grabs the emotions, and unleashes the spirit. Many young people are gifted musicians and readily offer their gifts when those gifts are appreciated.

Inviting youth to create music as a worship experience capitalizes on their God-given gifts for building up the body of Christ. Youth can create music in many different ways for different kinds of worship experiences.

1. Perform the songs. Although this is the most obvious way to create music, it is not always the easiest.

- Begin with simple songs and use songs that lend themselves to hand-clapping rhythm. It is often easier to get involved both physically and verbally.
- Teach the songs. Often youth don't sing because they don't know the words or the tune. It is important not to assume, but to teach both and then repeat the song until it is learned. It is also best to teach only one or two songs at a time.
- Cultivate the gifts of those who love to sing by inviting them to help lead and teach. Someone in the youth group might be willing to learn guitar if invited.

2. Write the songs.

- An easy way for youth to write songs is to utilize the very old technique of Christianizing the words to an existing song. Many cherished hymns started out this way.
- Youth can go beyond changing a few words and phrases; they can write completely new lyrics to familiar tunes.
- One simple technique is to create a poem that tells a story about someone's experience or ideas. Then invite a musician to compose a simple tune to fit the poem.
- Another good learning experience can come from trying to update songs, either by speaking to current events or issues, changing archaic or offensive language, or adjusting the theology of a song.

3. Appreciate the songs. Youth are often open to many kinds of music but familiar with only a few styles. Introducing youth to more musical forms and styles can increase their interest in music.

- Listen to and sing musical forms that youth rarely hear, such as jazz, gospel, contemporary Christian, bluegrass, country, or rock.
- Introduce music from other cultures. African, Jamaican, and Latin American music is often easier to learn and sing because it is more dependent on the voice than instruments.
- Invite music experts to come and teach youth about music—what it is, how it works, where it comes from, and the contribution it has made in life, history, and the church.

Too often youth sponsors ignore music because they think they have to be musicians to include music in their ministry. But music is so much a part of our lives that all of us are experienced with music to some degree. It's worth the effort to find ways to make music with your youth.

CHAPTER 19
RETREAT FOR SPIRITUAL GROWTH

On a warm Sunday morning in August, Hilary opened a hand-written letter from the youth group chair asking her to be the new youth sponsor. She smiled and her mind quickly jumped back to her youth group's weekend trip to the mountains twenty years ago. She remembered the weather was magnificent—the air still and crisp as fresh snow fell. She remembered the warm smells—a fire burning and popcorn popping. She remembered a song—a guitar coming to life and everyone beginning to sing. And she remembered the sense of God's presence—a flood of memories from a weekend retreat that had changed her life and the life of her youth group.

Though perhaps romantic, this story offers a glimpse of the powerful spiritual experience youth can have on a retreat.

For many youth, the busyness of everyday life overwhelms their ability to hear "the still, small voice of God." Homework, practices, work schedules, family responsibilities, recreation and entertainment, social life, and even church activities make it difficult to find a quiet time and a place to retreat, listen, and hear God. Retreating from busyness to a camp or retreat center can give youth the space to hear God's call on their lives or ponder the deep questions of faith or enjoy being together as God's children. In retreat settings, Hilary's story is often not far from the truth.

> **"LET'S GO TO A QUIET PLACE**
>
> —Jesus, Mark 6:31

Retreats can serve at least three purposes. In your planning, first determine the purpose for your retreat.

GROW THE BODY

1. *Build community.* For many groups, the greatest need for a retreat may be to build a sense of group identity and unity. Especially at the beginning of the youth group year, a retreat can be an excellent way to welcome new youth, get acquainted, and begin building relationships of caring and trust.

2. *Break routine.* Retreating breaks the grind of daily routines. Fasting from watches and schedules, junk food and junk entertainment, primping and posturing can be refreshing.

3. *Be youth.* Having fun, playing new and/or noncompetitive games, and freeing the child can be liberating for youth who are often living adult-like lives. A retreat can provide a safe place to still be a kid.

GROW THE MIND

1. *Meet an issue.* Youth are faced with a multitude of complicated and confusing issues. A retreat provides the time and space to explore tough issues.

2. *Make decisions.* A retreat provides an excellent opportunity for planning the youth group year. With the leadership team or the entire youth group, bring schedules, worksheets, budgets, and ideas for a weekend or a day of decision making.

3. *Mark turning points.* Driving licenses, graduations, tragedies, conversion experiences, vocational decisions, college choices, and other important moments in the lives of youth can all be marked by a retreat experience. Some of these turning points invite celebration, others invite mourning, and others invite exploration, challenge, and decisions. The retreat can establish rituals and traditions that give meaning, depth, and significance to the important experiences of youth.

GROW THE SPIRIT

1. *Seek God.* Many youth testify that their closest moments with God occurred in retreat settings. Getting away into the serenity of God's creation invites youth into an unusual silence where they can both seek God and hear God. By focusing on prayer, Bible reading, or other spiritual disciplines in a retreat, youth find the time to encounter Christ.

2. *Solidify commitments.* Many youth point to retreats as the places where they decided to follow Christ and serve the church. Invitations to faith, to service, to mission, and to new heights of discipleship are usually welcome in the retreat setting.

The next big question in retreat planning is how to accomplish the purpose. The best way to work at this is to invite the retreat planning team to a brainstorming session. Post your purpose on a wall and then throw out every idea you can think of that might help accomplish the purpose. Special speakers, video presentations, curriculum, skits, hikes, special meals, quiet periods, and service are common retreat experiences. The only requirement is that every activity needs to contribute to the purpose of the retreat.

After deciding on your activities, outline a schedule, secure the necessary resources, determine a place and a time, and assign responsibilities.

A retreat can turn out to be just another piece of the busyness that plagues the lives of youth and youth sponsors. To help you avoid that, post the following list on the wall next to your brainstorming list.

Quick Tip
CONVENANTING THE RETREAT EXPERIENCE

Most youth sponsors worry about discipline issues during retreat experiences. One helpful way to minimize problems is to create a covenant for the experience and ask each participant to prayerfully decide if he or she can sign and keep the covenant. It can be as simple as two or three sentences. The three essential components of the covenant are the purpose for the retreat, a personal statement of commitment to keep the covenant, and a place to sign. Most youth respond well to this invitation to responsibility and accountability.

SIX KEYS TO RETREATING FOR SPIRITUAL GROWTH

S implify. Retreat means keeping everything from meals to travel to activities as simple as possible.

P lay. Retreat means that in a world of work, we make time to play and release the childlikeness that Jesus invited.

I nterrupt. Retreat means getting away from the rigors, routines, and rigidity of daily life.

R elax. Retreat means making space for a restful, quiet, and non-busy period of time.

I lluminate. Retreat means inviting new ways of seeing God, the world, others, and faith.

T antalize. Retreat means inviting the unexpected, whether planned or unplanned.

YOUTH GROUP RETREAT
COVENANT FORM

Event name:_____   Date: _____

Purpose of the Retreat:
- _____
- _____
- _____

Covenant Agreements:

1. _____
2. _____
3. _____
4. _____
5. _____

I, _____, agree to support the purpose of this retreat through
my attendance, my participation, and my wilingness to abide by the
covenant agreements.

We/I, _____, as parent(s) of _____, understand the
purpose of this retreat and its covenant agreements. We/I understand that
all the participants will live together at the retreat according to these
guidelines.

We/I, _____, as parent(s) of _____, hereby grant
permission to _____, our youth group leader, to seek
medical aid for _____ in the event of accident of illness.

Phone Numbers: _____   Date: _____

Insurance Company: _____   No: _____

CHAPTER 20
WORSHIP
WITH YOUTH

As the youth group filed into the room, a boom box was playing Colombian instrumental music played on traditional instruments. As soon as the last person sat down, Sharon stood up and shouted, "El Espiritu creador de Dios esta en el mundo!" Then Kathy stood up and shouted, "God's creative Spirit is in the world!" Immediately, a sense of expectation that God would soon be encountered filled the room. After readings, songs, prayer, and a sermon/slide presentation, almost all the youth present knew that God had spoken, and they had had a chance to hear.

Worship with youth may be one of the greatest challenges facing adults in ministry with youth groups, yet it is one of the most important elements of youth group ministry. Worship, in its broadest sense, happens whenever a person encounters God and is touched by God's presence, love, and power. But in a narrower sense, worship is when believers, young and old, gather to focus their attention upon God and what God has done for them and the world through Jesus Christ. This focus is achieved through songs, prayers, the Word, readings, the Lord's Supper, and other elements of worship. This is corporate worship.

Many youth experienced worship only on Sunday mornings in the context of the whole congregation. Occasionally, the youth group may worship together on a retreat or a service experience. But rarely do youth groups formally worship at their regular gathering times. Even if corporate worship has not been a regular part of your youth group gatherings, it can be and should be. Creating a quarterly or monthly youth group gathering just for worship is a good beginning.

Every experience of corporate worship should serve three goals:

The first goal: worship focuses on God and God's salvation for the world. The purpose of Christian worship is to draw attention to God. Therefore, every theme that is chosen for worship must be connected in some way to the person of God or the saving action of God in the world. Themes can be inspired by current events, the seasons of the year or the church year, or crucial experiences and issues in church life. The theme chosen should direct attention to God and God's acts of salvation. If worship is directed anywhere else, it cannot be Christian.

The second goal: worship pays attention to the world. For youth this means that worship allows them to bare their souls, the pain and sorrow, the triumph and joy, the sin and forgiveness, the despair and the hope. Worship that doesn't listen to the real world of everyday life is shallow and meaningless.

> **"WORSHIP**
>
> **IS THE GOSPEL**
>
> **IN MOTION."**
>
> —Robert Webber, *YouthWorker* 7:4, p. 25

The third goal: worship pays attention to the worshiper. Real worship invites participation. Youth are not interested in worship that does not engage them or allow expression. Worship must be active, it must move, it must ignite a fire if it is going to change lives.

How can worship with youth meet these goals? In the chapter "Dig into Bible Study," five elements for designing a Bible study experience were identified. These same elements, approached from a slightly different angle, also provide an outline for designing a worship experience with youth.

1. **Focus** attention on the theme. Every worship experience should have a central identifiable theme that directs attention to God or God's acts. The first activity of the worship experience should identify the chosen theme, invite attention, and create expectation. In many ways, this first element is the most crucial part of the experience.

2. **Connect** the theme to the life experience of the youth group. At this point, youth need to see that this worship experience will be relevant, worthy of their attention.

3. **Dig** into the theme by listening and interpreting Scripture. Every worship experience should include interaction with the Word of God. This is God's opportunity to speak to youth in the conversation of worship.

4. **Re-connect** the theme back to the life experience of youth. Again, the goal is to make what has been heard from God's Word on the theme relevant for everyday life. This element often presents the greatest challenge for the leader.

5. **Respond** by inviting youth to make a decision to actively let God know that they have been touched by their encounter. Worship is always a two-way conversation. God speaks to those who worship, and those who worship speak to God.

Within these five elements of a worship experience, any number of activities can be used. Traditionally, worship includes music, prayer, preaching, Scripture readings, litanies, and offerings. But it can also include slide presentations, mime, reader's theater, clowning, skits, video, stories, body sculpture, monologue, dance, art, drama, and more. In addition, worship can take place in many settings, including in a cemetery, in a restaurant, in a cave, on a bus, by the sea, in a jail cell, in an attic, and more. Worship can also take into consideration how all the five senses are involved. Imagination is a key ingredient in creative worship.

Above all else, worship requires preparation. It is not enough to run into a bookstore to find a skit book, throw a few songs and prayers together, read a meditation from a devotional book, and call that worship. Rather, every element should point to God through the theme, relate to the real world, and involve every youth who is worshipping. Worship invites youth to look at their lives, encounter and listen to God, then go out with a new commitment to love and serve God faithfully. It is a serious experience that requires prayerful preparation, but it has the power to change not only the lives of youth but the life of the youth group as well.

CHAPTER 21
TRAIN WORSHIP LEADERS

The congregation waited in the sanctuary, anticipating an unusual worship service. Pete and Kaye and the youth group waited in the fellowship hall, worrying about what would be sung, what would be prayed, and what would be said. No one knew quite what to expect. The service began and proceeded just as it had been planned. When it was over, the youth breathed a sigh of relief, Pete and Kaye quit sweating, and Abe, the church custodian, walked over and told them it was the best worship he had experienced in years.

> **"IN WORSHIP,**
> **GOD TOUCHES THE CORE OF OUR**
> **BEING, AND WE ARE CHANGED.**
> **LET US NOW PREPARE FOR GOD'S TOUCH."**
> —G. Temp Sparkman, *Writing Your Own Worship Materials*, p. 19

Youth Sunday. The words strike dread into the hearts of most volunteer youth sponsors, but it doesn't have to. Too often Youth Sundays are thrown together at the last minute. Youth are asked to find resources and they don't. Youth say they will come, and then they don't show up. Finally the youth sponsors pick up the pieces, and they feel roped. The solution, though, is simple: early preparation.

STEP 1: SET A DATE FOR YOUTH SUNDAY THREE MONTHS AHEAD.

Weeks go by faster than most people realize, especially when meetings can happen only once or twice a week. Setting a date early gives everyone a chance to mark their calendars, adequately prepare, and begin praying for God's Spirit to be present in your decisions and your preparations.

STEP 2: TWO MONTHS AHEAD, CREATE A THREE- TO FIVE-PERSON WORSHIP PREPARATION TEAM.

Worship is much easier to prepare in a small group. This team should meet immediately and make three decisions:

1. Determine a theme for the worship service.
2. Define an order of worship activities incorporating the five worship elements—focus, connect, dig, re-connect, and respond. These can be used within the traditional worship order of the congregation or in a new worship order.
3. Make assignments to the members of the preparation team to begin finding or writing resources.

> **Quick Tip**
> The five elements of worship in the traditional worship order:
> **Focus**
> • Prelude
> • Call to Worship
> • Opening Prayer
> **Connect**
> • Songs
> • Readings
> **Dig**
> • Scripture
> • Sermon
> **Re-connect**
> • Songs
> • Testimonies
> **Respond**
> • Offerings
> • Announcements
> • Benediction

STEP 3: ONE MONTH BEFORE THE WORSHIP SERVICE, TWO DECISIONS NEED TO BE MADE:

1. A final order of worship activities should be written up identifying the resources to be used for each activity.
2. Assignments should be made to the persons who will lead and participate in each worship activity.

STEP 4: TWO WEEKS BEFORE YOUTH SUNDAY, GATHER TOGETHER ALL THE LEADERS AND PARTICIPANTS IN THE WORSHIP SERVICE AND WALK THROUGH THE SERVICE.

This will encourage the leaders and participants to have their preparations complete and will help the youth feel more comfortable doing activities they probably rarely do. And, it will help you work out any glitches that show up. Also, take time to pray together for the worship service, those who will lead and participate, and those who will be attending.

STEP 5: ONE WEEK BEFORE YOUTH SUNDAY, REPEAT STEP FOUR.

STEP 6: WORSHIP THE LORD!

STEP 7: REST.

This is what your pastor does after worship.

Youth are incredibly capable, creative, and gifted people. When it is well-prepared, youth-led worship often invites the kind of responses Abe shared. Youth can bring an energy, passion, and faith to worship that renews everyone, young and old. So when Youth Sunday comes, prepare to worship the Lord.

> ### Quick Tip
> Try to help find ways for youth to be involved regularly in leading and participating in worship. Youth who do this are better prepared when Youth Sunday comes around, and it won't feel like a token experience.

TEN IDEAS FOR CREATIVE WORSHIP PREPARATION

1. Use the Bible study or Sunday school curriculum as a resource for worship activities focusing on the same theme.
2. Ask the pastor to visit the youth group and explain the meanings of the different worship activities.
3. Do a dress rehearsal of the Youth Sunday worship service in a home for the elderly.
4. When using radically innovative worship activity in the worship service, such as clowning or dance, use only one such activity in a service and make sure it is well prepared so people can learn to appreciate innovations rather than be threatened by them.
5. Attend worship in other congregations to discover what they do differently.
6. In designing worship activities, be sensitive to those who may be hearing or visually impaired. Find creative ways to help them experience the worship that has been prepared.
7. Use clothing, color, symbols, smells, and sounds to enhance the worship experience. For example, bake bread in the fellowship hall with a theme like "Jesus: The Bread of Life."
8. When used in brief and appropriate ways, video can be an incredible asset to worship. On the other hand, you may prefer to make worship a time to retreat from the media.
9. Take the risk of writing worship materials. It is not difficult to rewrite Scripture into reader's theater or to write prayers. Some youth are gifted songwriters. The church is a place where these gifts should be cultivated.
10. Read chapter 20, "Worship with Youth," for more ideas that might work in youth-led worship.

YOUTH GROUP
BIBLE STUDY PLANNING WORKSHEET

Lesson Title: _____

Date: _____

Scripture: _____

Goals:
- _____
- _____

TRADITIONAL ELEMENTS	WORSHIP ACTIVITIES	WORSHIP RESOURCES
Focus • Prelude • Call to worship • Opening Prayer		
Connect • Songs • Readings • Drama		
Dig • Scripture presentation • Sermon/meditation		
Re-Connect • Songs • Testimonies • Work of the Church		
Respond • Offerings • Announcements • Benediction		

PART 3
COMM-
MUN-
ITY

CHAPTER 22
FORM A GROUP IDENTITY

Sandy has fond memories of her youth group experience. She remembers a level of peer-caring—a sense of group identity—that would be the envy of most youth sponsors. Now, as a youth pastor, she longs for this kind of caring among the youth in her church, but it just isn't happening. Though the youth all go to the same high school, they spend little time together at school. Many are just acquaintances, and during youth group activities, they often act as if they don't want to be together. Sandy is losing hope that the kind of intimate sharing and caring she remembers will ever happen in this group.

Building group identity in the youth group takes time.

Some youth may have not yet made a commitment to follow Jesus Christ. Others may be new Christians. Some may be struggling with whether they really want to live the Christian life. A few may be wrestling with specific issues. And there are always a few youth whose faith commitment is a model for everyone. More often than not, when there are wide differences in faith commitment, some youth will be at the core of the group and others will be on the fringe.

> ## "COMMUNITY
> ### IS CURRENTLY RARE."
>
> —M. Scott Peck, A Different Drum, p. 25

The sense of group identity Sandy hopes for grows out of a shared commitment to Christ and to each other as the body of Christ. Many youth simply are not there yet. Group-building activities that assume a deep level of commitment may be considered manipulative and intrusive by youth not ready to become too intimate with the group. If that happens, those activities can do more harm than good. Any attempt to build community within the group must take into account the different places youth are in their faith journeys. This requires coming to terms with several realities:

REALITY 1: WHEN YOUTH LEAVE THE GROUP AND NEW YOUTH ENTER, THE GROUP CHANGES.

This means that each year, building group identity must begin again.

REALITY 2: EACH YEAR'S GROUP HAS DIFFERENT NEEDS.

To make the youth group a setting where those needs can be addressed, you need to know the youth, their families, and their life situations. When you know their interests, skills, problems, hopes, and fears, you are better able to design youth group experiences that address their needs. Sometimes conducting a survey can be helpful.

REALITY 3: ONCE YOU HAVE IDENTIFIED NEEDS, YOUTH GROUP PROGRAMMING CAN BEGIN TO ADDRESS THOSE NEEDS, BUT THIS SHOULD BE DONE GRADUALLY.

In the beginning, gathering for social interaction with minimal attention to faith and personal needs may be best. Fun, nonthreatening, life-enhancing activities help youth discover that the youth group is a safe place to be honest and open—to be themselves. Later, as connections between the youth develop, you can focus more on issues and topics that address the needs of the youth. As needs are met, youth feel the care and compassion of the group. Eventually, youth can be challenged with the call to follow Jesus Christ. Youth who have grown up in the church may need this invitation as much as new participants. Finally, the youth group may become a discipling community that worships together, cares for one another, and shares with the larger community outside the youth group.

REALITY 4: RECOGNIZE THAT NOT EVERY YOUTH GROUP WILL REACH THIS GOAL, AND THAT IS OKAY.

Their experience may have started them on the journey. While few youth groups attain this ideal in one year, it is still an ideal worth pursuing.

In light of these realities, here are several strategies that can help build group identity in the youth group setting:

- **Be a welcoming group.** Ask core members of the group to be the unofficial welcomers—always welcoming new youth and reaching out to those on the fringe. In discussions, ask for everyone's point of view, or create smaller groups so everyone feels heard and can contribute.

- **Teach listening, conversational, and welcoming skills to the core members of the youth group.** Many youth don't know how to listen attentively, ask questions, or start a conversation with a new person. These skills are essential for helping new youth feel a part of the youth group.

- **Plan activities in which all group members can succeed.** Youth who lose in a competitive activity or who are not able to participate—physically challenged persons, for example—will be easily discouraged from deeper involvement in the youth group. Inclusive activities and inclusive language are the rule of the day in our society, and youth are acutely sensitive to being excluded.

- **Worship together.** Allow the Holy Spirit to draw youth together through common experiences of spiritual life. Even in the early life of the youth group, worship experiences of music, prayer, reflection, journaling, and sharing can help to build a common focus on God, a caring concern for one another, and compassion for others.

Building the "group" in youth group is an important task of youth ministry. It doesn't happen automatically and it doesn't happen overnight. But, with careful planning, attention, and nurture, youth sponsors can help their youth groups develop a sense of community that youth like Sandy will cherish the rest of their lives.

CHAPTER 23
WELCOME EVERYONE

The town was changing and Randy and Karen were experiencing it firsthand. Families from the city were moving to their rural community to escape the drugs, gangs, and violence. The youth from these families began showing up at youth group Bible studies. The way they dressed was different, the way they talked was different, and even what they believed was different.

Any group, whether youth or adult, has a tendency to close ranks, shut the doors, become a clique. Some people call this community. It may be community of some kind, but it isn't Christian community. The Christian community must be a place where all kinds of people are welcomed regardless of who they are, where they come from, or what they look like. The youth group, if it is to be a Christian youth group, can be no exception. Randy and Karen knew this; now they had to practice it.

Welcoming everyone—new youth, fringe youth, youth of different ages, youth with different backgrounds, youth with special needs—can be a challenge, but it is not an insurmountable one. It does, however, require paying attention, adjusting, and learning to know these youth so the group can welcome them into the community and minister to them. Keeping three principles in mind will help:

PRINCIPLE 1: COMMIT TO BE A WELCOMING GROUP.

Youth are no different than adults. Given a choice, they prefer to be with people they know. So, for a youth group to welcome people who are different, the group must make an intentional choice. Becoming a welcoming group may require a special meeting of the core members of the youth group to talk about inclusivity. It may require teaching on how to welcome people who are different. And it may require changes in programming that recognize the needs and interests of the different youth now participating in the youth group. But first, it requires a decision to be a welcoming youth group.

PRINCIPLE 2: MODEL AND CULTIVATE WELCOMING SKILLS.

Youth who are different usually come to a youth group meeting for one of three reasons. First, they may have been invited by one of the core youth group members. Second, youth may come out of curiosity to test how welcoming your youth group may be. This, at least, suggests an interest in being connected to the church. Third, youth may visit because parents or other relatives made them come. These youth present the youth group with an opportunity to give the surprise gift of inclusiveness.

When youth sponsors welcome these visitors, their example teaches

> **"THERE** ARE ALWAYS TWO GROUPS OF YOUTH WITH WHOM WE CAN MINISTER: THOSE WITHIN THE CHURCH AND THOSE WE HAVE NOT YET INVITED."

and encourages the regular members of the youth group to be welcoming. Even if the youth in the youth group are welcoming, when youth sponsors are not, most visitors will not come back.

PRINCIPLE 3: WATCH FOR BARRIERS THAT CAN EXCLUDE PEOPLE.

One way to do this is to imagine yourself in the shoes of different youth. Can a youth who uses a wheelchair get to where you meet? Can a nonhearing youth see people when they talk or can an interpreter be provided? If a youth is from a different cultural background, can she hear her language in the songs, or see her culture on posters and videos? If a youth is from a family with low or fluctuating income, is he at risk of feeling excluded or embarrassed when group members, either formally or informally, are expected to share the expense of a group activity or a trip to a restaurant? Can youth from outside the church understand the code language and assumed knowledge of your Christian community? Most youth will not notice these details, so youth sponsors must learn to watch for them.

These three principles can guide your youth group as you develop strategies for becoming a welcoming community of youth.

SIX WELCOMING STRATEGIES:

1. Meet people at the door. This may seem corny at first, but many youth feel like nobody cares if they show up. Meeting youth as they enter insures that every person is noticed and spoken to at least once.

2. Assign a welcoming team. Ask several extrovert youth from the youth group to be a team that looks for new persons, starts conversations, and invites them to participate in activities.

3. Follow up. Either the youth sponsors or the welcoming team can follow up youth who visit the youth group. Greet them in school or in the community, ask them if they enjoyed their visit, and invite them back. For youth who are different, follow-up can be the real test of whether you want their presence or whether you tolerated their presence.

4. Make adjustments. Especially for youth with physical challenges, making adjustments to accommodate their ability goes a long way toward making them feel welcome.

5. Neither highlight nor ignore differences. Most youth who are different, for whatever reason, know they are different. They usually know you are more uncomfortable than they are. Noticing differences in a nonjudgmental way can express acceptance. Ignoring differences can sometimes be just as cruel as ridiculing them.

6. Eat together. Eating is a common experience everyone can share. If different youth are coming occasionally, it might be good to begin youth group gatherings with snacks. This helps to break down barriers, ease tensions, and find common ground.

Just make sure the welcoming team is functioning so people aren't left eating by themselves.

Many more strategies can be devised to help your youth group become a welcoming community, but most important is simply deciding to be a welcoming youth group. At the very least, it is a response of gratefulness by those already in the youth group. At the most, it is a sign of the presence of the kingdom.

CHAPTER 24
FACILITATE
FRIENDSHIP

Sally was one of three freshmen entering the youth group in September. Marlene, one of the youth sponsors and Sally's mentor, was concerned about how Sally would be integrated into the youth group. She called a meeting of the leadership team and suggested that three youth already in the youth group volunteer to create an intentional friendship with each of the three incoming freshmen. The leadership team thought this was a great idea, three youth were eager to give it a try, and when Sally walked into the first youth group gathering, she was immediately welcomed by Michele, a junior, who would soon become Sally's good friend, guide to high school life, and confidant.

Unlike Sally and Michele, most youth enter friendships incidentally. Through a chance encounter at church, in the neighborhood, during extracurricular activities, in a class, or on the job, the possibility for a friendship is born. Yet, developing such a chance encounter into a friendship is a creative act. The youth must talk together, discover things they have in common, and find ways to spend time together. Even when the first encounter is unintentional, a friendship is created unintentionally.

> ## "THERE IS
> ### NOTHING MORE MOVING
> ### IN LIFE THAN TO HEAR SOMEONE
> ### SAY, 'I NEED YOU.'"
>
> —William Barclay, *Daily Celebration*, p. 131

No community in the youth group is the result of youth creating intentional friendships. There are four levels of friendship:

1. *Casual acquaintances.* Co-workers, classmates, and others one knows and sees occasionally.

2. *Casual friends.* The larger group of people who hang out together and do things together from time to time.

3. *Close friends.* Those with whom secrets are shared, who listen to problems, and who can be counted on in an emergency.

4. *Intimate friends.* Friends forever, the people whose love is so deep they might even die for one another.

Within the youth group, some or all levels of friendship may be functioning. Very large youth groups may include youth who aren't even acquainted with each other. But all youth groups will want to help youth create and move into deeper friendships so they can become a stronger caring community of faith. Not every relationship needs to become intimate, but acquaintance friendships are not enough.

Intentional friendships are developed much the same way friendships develop naturally:

STEP 1: MAKE FRIEND-MAKING A PRIORITY.

A core of people in the youth group need to decide that creating intentional friendships is important for the youth group. It isn't up to the newcomers or fringe youth to take the initiative; it is the responsibility of core members of the group. Once the group makes this commitment, the leadership team or youth sponsors need to recruit youth in the group who are willing to open themselves up to new friendships.

STEP 2: START CONVERSATIONS.

Although many youth are able to do this naturally, it is more difficult to do it intentionally. Taking the first step to walk up to a stranger, even in the peer group, involves risk. It calls for asking questions and listening, both skills that have to be learned and practiced. And it involves a commitment to continue friendships once they are started. Role playing is a safe way to practice the conversational skills needed for creating friendships.

STEP 3: LOOK FOR COMMON GROUND.

Common ground can be based on anything—hobbies, favorite studies, personal history, job or vocational interest, travels, faith experiences, extracurricular involvements, family connections, future hopes, books, music, or movies. Even similar difficult experiences can provide common ground for creating a friendship.

STEP 4: INVEST TIME.

Committing time to creating a friendship is as intentional as the decision to have the first conversation. Doing things together and talking together are the soil for growing any friendship that goes beyond acquaintance.

STEP 5: WATCH THE FRIENDSHIP GROW.

With the intentional investment of time, acquaintance friendship grows into casual friendship, and the new friend begins to experience community in the youth group.

Creating intentional friendships is a peer activity. Youth sponsors, however, play the crucial role of bringing the idea to the core youth of the group. Youth sponsors can insure that training in conversational skills is offered, and they can help to plan youth group activities where intentional friendships can be cultivated.

Finally, youth sponsors can model the importance of intentional friendships. To teach youth to be creative friend-makers is to give the gift of a lifetime.

CHAPTER 25
HEAL THE PAIN

Linda and her sister were out for a bike ride when a car came out of nowhere, and Linda was gone. The youth group would never again see her sparkling smile. They would never again hear her contagious laugh. Linda was gone.

Every youth will experience tragedy firsthand—the death of a family member or friend, a debilitating disease or accident, a divorce or some other family trauma, a natural disaster or a national crisis, a family scandal, or a personal failure. When tragedy strikes, whether the experience touches just one person or involves the entire group as Linda's death did, youth need to be able to count on youth sponsors and the youth group for support. How can youth sponsors guide the youth group in responding to tragedy in ways that offer comfort and healing? Here are six possible responses:

THE FIRST RESPONSE: COME TOGETHER.

Whether the tragedy is experienced by an individual or the whole group, the first appropriate youth group response is to gather. Youth who face tragedy need to know they won't have to face it alone. Determining when to meet for this first gathering needs to depend on the personal agenda of those most directly affected. Family meetings, meetings with the pastor or a counselor, or other issues may have to take priority over a youth group gathering. This first youth group gathering can be either a normal meeting time or, if it is better, a special meeting time. In some cases it may be appropriate to meet at the person's home, or it may be best to use the youth group's normal meeting place. However the first gathering occurs, the surroundings should be familiar and provide the freedom for intimacy.

THE SECOND RESPONSE: TAKE TIME FOR QUIET AND SHARING.

Most of the time, youth in grief only need others to be present with them. Youth sponsors may assure the youth group that silence is okay, even encouraged. At the same time, sharing is also appropriate. Often youth feel unsure about what to say. Expressions of empathy—tears, holding hands, hugs, and words of love, care, and concern—are always appropriate. Steer conversation away from suggesting reasons for the tragedy and analyzing what happened. You can assure youth that God grieves with them.

> **"MINISTRY TO YOUTH IS BEST DONE BY OTHER YOUTH."**
>
> —Jim Burns, as quoted by Joan Sturkie and Siang-Yan Tan in *Advanced Peer Counseling in Youth Groups*, p. 9

THE THIRD RESPONSE: EXPLAIN THE GRIEF PROCESS.

Many youth (and adults) do not understand how grief works, so are confused by their own emotions. Youth sponsors can teach or invite someone else to teach the youth group about grief and how the grief process leads to healing. Opportunities to respond to teaching through sharing, prayer, or journaling can contribute to the healing process.

THE FOURTH RESPONSE: WALK ALONGSIDE YOUTH.

Everyone recovers from a tragedy at different rates, and no one recovers overnight. There are many ways to express caring during the healing process—cards of encouragement, phone calls, locker notes, prayers (both public and private), help with meals and other daily chores, and words of remembrance.

THE FIFTH RESPONSE: CONSIDER A MEMORIAL.

One way to permanently remember and honor the tragedy is to memorialize it or the person. This should be a careful decision; not all tragedies can or should be memorialized. If there is interest in doing this, it should be done in consultation with those most directly affected.

Quick Tip

Don't wait for a tragedy to happen. Since virtually all youth will experience tragedy, why not prepare for it ahead of time? Learn about the grieving process, imagine how the youth group would respond to different tragic experiences, and train youth in basic helping skills. Group preparation, including role playing, can assure youth that their youth group will be community for them when tragedy comes.

THE FINAL RESPONSE: GO ON WITH LIFE.

At some point, grieving must be left behind and life must go on. This moment can be signaled by the start of new year, a memorial, the anniversary of the tragedy, or just an acknowledgment that things are back to normal and that is okay. This does not mean the tragedy is forgotten, but that healing has taken place.

Jesus' crucifixion was a tragedy. It didn't happen because God desired it. Jesus, in Gethsemane, intensely wished to avoid it. Yet, God used the tragedy of Jesus' death to bring salvation, healing, and hope to the world. Similarly, tragedy can provide salvation, healing, and hope for the youth group as well—maybe not in such a cosmic way, but in a very human and a very Christian way. When salvation, healing, and hope arise out of tragedy, the youth group can experience Spirit-inspired community.

CHAPTER 26
CELEBRATE LIFE-MARKERS

Dillon was ecstatic. After all the practice, all the anticipation, all the tension, he had passed the tests. He had his driver's license. Now he had power, control, independence. He was grown-up—well, at least close.

In North American society, the driver's license is an important life-marker. From the time children are able to imagine driving a car, they anticipate the moment when they will be able to drive. Getting a driver's license is a sign of coming of age. It represents beginning the transition into the adult world. It signals growing independence. Yet, for all of its importance in the lives of youth, rarely does the church recognize this life-marker. It is all but ignored by the very community that speaks repeatedly of its concern for its youth. It is no surprise that youth sometimes describe the church as irrelevant and unconcerned.

The youth group is a setting where important life-markers can be celebrated. We live in a society where only superstars get noticed. The rest live anonymously—silent spectators, sometimes worshippers, of the mostly undeserving heroes of popular culture.

Our youth don't need to feel anonymous. When we acknowledge and celebrate life-markers, we honor youth. We recognize and validate their worth as persons.

The benefits of celebrating life-markers are multiplied as that acknowledgment motivates youth:

- Life-changing decisions are easier to make when they are recognized and cherished.
- Commitments are easier to uphold when others celebrate their beginning and their fulfillment.

- It is more exciting to explore new opportunities when encouraged by others.
- Self-esteem grows when peers and adults honor developmental changes and life achievements.
- Attitudes about faith, people, and the world become more positive when celebrating the lives of others.

At least nine life-markers can be celebrated during the teen years. Six of these have to do with "being" and are experienced by most youth. Three have to do with "doing." They are activities and accomplishments that some youth experience and others do not. When celebrating life-markers, it is important to keep a balance between "being" and "doing" markers.

LIFE-MARKERS OF "BEING"

1. Passing into puberty. The profound physical, emotional, relational, and spiritual changes that youth experience during puberty are too often ignored. These changes are very personal and may best be celebrated privately with a parent or other adult relative, an older sibling, or a mentor. Sensitive public celebrations within genders can also be appropriate in some cases. The celebrations can center around the first shave, the onset of menstruation, the voice change, or the acknowledgment of sexual interest.

2. Graduation. For many youth, the moves from grade 8 into high school and from high school to college or the work world are among the most profound social changes they experience. The schools often celebrate these moves with great fanfare. The church and the youth group can also acknowledge the change and pledge their support and encouragement for the coming years.

> **"VERY** FEW YOUNG PEOPLE TAKE THEIR LIFE SERIOUSLY ENOUGH TO WANT TO TALK ABOUT IT."
>
> —Michael Warren, *Youth, Gospel, Liberation*, p. 20

3. Birthdays. Perhaps the easiest opportunities to recognize youth and celebrate who they are becoming are their birthdays. In this culture, the sixteenth and the eighteenth birthdays are recognized as steps to greater responsibility in society.

4. Driver's license. The opportunity to sit behind a ton of steel and drive it at 55 mph is a responsibility rarely acknowledged as a gift of power. Yet, every youth knows it is exactly that. When that power is celebrated within the community, youth can become more aware of their responsibility for their use of that power within the community.

5. Confession of faith and baptism. This milestone should be a focal point, not just a postscript to the Sunday morning worship service. Acceptance of Christ and the community of faith is a life-and-death decision. The way we acknowledge and celebrate that choice should reflect that.

6. Anniversaries. Certain experiences become life-markers for those who go through them. The trauma of a death or divorce, the recovery from an accident or a disease, a victory over an addiction or a disorder are experiences that can be sensitively acknowledged and appropriately celebrated in ways that further healthy healing. The individuals are always aware of these anniversaries; their closest faith community, the youth group, should be too.

LIFE-MARKERS OF "DOING"

7. School and personal achievements. These life-markers are important, but they present problems in our society. Too often they are the only life-markers of youth that are celebrated. Often they are celebrated for questionable reasons and in ways that exclude others. At the same time, youth accomplish remarkable things and often glory in each other's accomplishments. When done in balanced and inclusive ways, celebrating school and personal achievements in the youth group helps youth keep those achievements within the perspective of God's kingdom.

8. Attainment of personal goals. Youth are very good at setting goals for personal, physical, or spiritual growth. They, like everyone else, struggle to meet their goals. When those goals and their fulfillment is acknowledged, youth gain self-confidence to continue growing and discovering what God has in store for them.

9. Continued service. A year is a long time for a fifteen-year-old, especially in a society where thirty seconds is worth a million dollars. When youth stick to a commitment for a year or two or four, the youth group should celebrate. Following through on a job, position of leadership, volunteer work, and even (for some youth) school can be a great accomplishment that provides an opportunity to honor the power and reward of commitment.

Dillon's excitement about his driver's license didn't wane on his way to the youth group gathering, but he wasn't prepared for the party he and two others received that evening. A special key ring, the signing of the SADD (Students Against Drunk Driving) certificate, and the pledge to wear seat belts made the experience even more memorable. Every time he enters a car, especially with other youth group members, he is reminded of the gift of their friendship and of the responsibility he has assumed for their safety.

CHAPTER 27
PREPARE FOR PROBLEMS

Phil and Tim were great guys when they were alone, but when they were together, well, everyone knew there would be trouble. The youth group was planning their annual service trip, and Bev and Rich, their youth sponsors, wondered if Phil and Tim would go. When the registrations came in, Phil and Tim's were stapled together, of course. Although they had misgivings, Rich and Bev knew they couldn't keep Phil and Tim from going. For better or worse, they were a part of the youth group.

By its very nature, ministry with youth includes youth like Phil and Tim. Virtually every youth group, small or large, has at least one or two goofballs, and, on occasion, a serious behavior crisis. The prospect of confronting such situations is sometimes enough to keep adults out of youth ministry. But such problems don't have to be intimidating. It is possible to take steps that can prevent many problems of this kind and make it easier to deal with those that do arise:

PREVENTING PROBLEMS
STEP 1: DEFINE THE BOUNDARIES.

Youth live with boundaries every day—at school and jobs, in extracurricular activities, sometimes even at home. Yet, youth groups are often reluctant to define boundaries. Youth sponsors may fear "scaring" youth off, or they may naively assume that youth will behave well just because they are with a church group.

All it takes is for one or two "goofballs" to act up to create big problems for everyone. That is why the youth leadership team needs to define the appropriate boundaries for youth group settings. A list of general expectations, such as respect, courtesy, and appropriate language, provides a good foundation for all youth group events. For specific activities and events, a second list of expectations particular to the setting and activity may be needed. In describing these expectations, stick to what is truly necessary and say it in positive language.

STEP 2: DEFINE THE CONSEQUENCES.

When inappropriate behavior creeps into a youth group activity, the youth involved often confess, then excuse, the behavior, saying they didn't realize how serious it was. If consequences were not defined along with the expectations, they are probably telling the truth. Youth need to know how serious the rules are. Therefore, for each expectation, determine a consequence appropriate to the expectation. Then inform the youth group.

STEP 3: CREATE A COVENANT.

Creating a covenant puts "teeth" into expectations and consequences and gives youth responsibility for guarding their own behavior. The covenant should be simple—a list of expectations and consequences, a pledge statement to respect the expectations, and a place for a signature and a date. Covenants are best used for special events and trips, but, if there are persistent problems, it may be a helpful part of the routine youth group experience.

CONFRONTING PROBLEMS

Even with good preparations for preventing problems, some will still come. Youth are youth, not adults. They are still learning about appropriate behavior and respect for the group experience. So when problems creep in, it is important to have a plan for confronting them. Matthew 18:15-17, loosely paraphrased, offers a four-part formula for confronting problems head-on:

1. "If a member of the youth group misbehaves against the group, go to that member alone, and in a quiet place, confront the misbehavior and expect an apology. If the member listens, rejoice and begin anew."

2. "If the youth group member does not listen, take one or two others and confront the member so there can be no misunderstanding about the expectations and the consequences."

3. "If the youth group member still refuses to listen, bring the issue to the leadership team and apply the consequences."

4. "If the member refuses to listen to the leadership team, then send the youth home until the next youth event or activity."

This gracious approach to confronting problems in the youth group provides several opportunities for the youth group member to apologize and return to the youth group experience. It delays applying consequences, giving the youth an opportunity to reconsider the behavior and make a new start. And in the context of a covenant, it treats each youth with respect, expecting him or her to own the commitment made and the violation of that commitment. Not included in this approach to discipline are immediate consequences, impatience, disrespect, shouting, demeaning language, physical punishment, and unjust consequences.

> **"THERE ARE**
>
> **NO PREPACKAGED,**
>
> **EASY SOLUTIONS**
>
> **TO EVERY SITUATION."**
>
> —Dwight Spotts and Dave Veerman,
> *Reaching Out to Troubled Youth*, p. 93

Finally, always follow up with youth who have had a problem. They need to know that occasional misbehavior will not ostracize them from the group. Grace and forgiveness are always better teachers than punishment.

Problems are always unpleasant and inconvenient. But, handled well, they provide opportunities for youth to learn and grow in faith and to experience community.

WHEN INTERVENTION IS NEEDED

Some problems are so serious that they require intervention from outside the youth group or even the church. Personal threats, acts of violence, and drinking or drug abuse may require professional intervention. In consultation with the pastor or other professionals, plan how to respond should a serious incident occur.

A FINAL CAUTION

Given the state of our society, youth sponsors should seek training in how to appropriately handle youth behavior problems. Striking youth, verbally abusing youth, and excluding youth can create problems, sometimes including legal problems, for youth sponsors. This makes it crucial to have clear policies defining expectations and consequences. It may also be wise to share these policies with the pastor and the church leadership.

CHAPTER 28
BUST BUSYNESS

Amy was incredible. A junior in high school, she started on the basketball team and the volleyball team and wrote for the school newspaper. She played piano, sometimes for the junior choir, and sang in the school choir, which, of course, helped her get a supporting role in the school musical. Since age 8, Amy had participated in 4-H, so in spring she had to prepare for the county fair. Through the year she worked ten to twelve hours a week and was vice-president of the youth group. She had only made it to four of the year's nine youth group gatherings. The question was, Could she be president of the youth group?

Youth sponsors and parents alike often complain about the busy schedules of youth. Often they are also asking, Why do church activities seem to be at the bottom of the list? School unapologetically demands the priority time of youth. From homework to athletics, class parties to play practices, most youth are inundated with school life. And today, more and more youth are working, often at jobs with odd hours and inflexible schedules. Plus, every normal youth needs hang-out time with friends.

> **"THE** SUPPLY OF OPPORTUNITY IN ANY ONE LIFETIME IS SMALL AND PRECIOUS."
>
> —Scott Simon, National Public Radio's *Morning Edition*

In the midst of these demands, both the family and the church compete, sometimes with each other, for the remainder of a busy young person's time. Often it feels like the busyness is out of control.

Interestingly enough, many youth also report frustration

with their busyness. Some even are bitter about the ways in which they feel manipulated by those who compete for their time and commitment. From their point of view, however, all the alternatives are appealing. Reluctant to pass up opportunities, youth search for control of their lives. Youth sponsors can help young people and their families bust the busyness syndrome to enjoy a more satisfying and less stressful life.

STEP 1: NAME THE PROBLEM

The place to start is for everyone involved—parents, teens, and youth sponsors—to acknowledge what is happening. Once everyone admits that the problem exists and that it needs to be addressed, plan a meeting including the youth, at least one parent of each teen, and the youth sponsors. Even this first step may require everyone to forego some other activity.

STEP 2: SIZE UP THE PROBLEM

Purchase a four-month write-on/wipe-off board. At the meeting, fill it up with the schedules of all the youth. It may be helpful to use a different color pen for school activities, work schedules, family time, and youth group gatherings. Begin by blocking out the school day and school activities in which most of the youth participate. Be careful here, asking rather than making assumptions. Not everyone goes to every football game. Second, block out regular church/youth group activities. Third, block out family times. Finally, note the work schedules, especially where they overlap for several youth. Write small!

STEP 3: ANALYZE THE PROBLEM.

When the calendar is full, divide into parent, youth, and youth sponsor groups. Invite everyone to look at the calendar and record their observations about which activities are getting the most time, which activities deserve the most time, and ways they wish the calendar were different. Ask each group to report their observations when everyone comes back together. This may be a difficult part of the exercise since the groups probably will not agree on what's most important and why.

STEP 4: CONFRONT THE PROBLEM.

After each group has been heard, talk about workable changes that everyone can live with. This means prioritizing activities. There are two keys to this process. First, acknowledge that a schedule that suits everyone is impossible and, second, it's okay if every person cannot be involved in everything. Sometimes youth just need to be assured that it is okay to miss something once in a while.

STEP 5: ASK FAMILIES TO COME TO GRIPS WITH THE PROBLEM.

The last step is homework. In the end, it is up to the youth and their families to make decisions about busyness. To encourage further work on the issue, provide each youth with a calendar of the year's youth activities. Then ask each family to sit down and add family activities, school activities, and work schedules. This exercise may not change things much, but it at least invites the family to be aware of priorities and busyness.

Youth busyness is clearly a problem of priorities and choices. Although the church, the family, the school, and the workplace may each demand priority, most youth know that one area is more important than the others from time to time. A group process like this can give youth an opportunity to clarify their priorities, not only from their own perspectives but also taking into account the perspectives of others who care about them.

> ### Quick Tip
>
> A key to facilitating this process is to have the youth group calendar worked out at the beginning of the youth group year, usually September. This will require youth sponsors and the leadership team to work hard at planning the schedule early. Even if activities are uncertain, include them. If they fall through, they can be replaced by some other gathering of the youth group. Planning early is crucial. If the youth group schedule isn't priority at the beginning of the year for leadership, it won't be priority for youth through the year.

CHAPTER 29
FOOT THE BILL

Sue was becoming increasingly frustrated by the never-ending fund-raising that plagued her youth group. Although they always came up with great ideas to do excellent things, money was always a problem. Plus, as each year went by, transportation, insurance, lodging, and meals kept getting more expensive. The decision Sue faced was to either cut back on the youth program or keep fund-raising. Neither option appealed to her.

Youth ministry costs money. Everyone agrees that youth need to experience service and mission to gain a vision for the difference they can make in the world. Everyone agrees that youth should attend conferences and youth events to get a sense of the larger community of faith.

> **"HOW** WE
> ———————
> **FINANCE YOUTH MINISTRY**
> ———————
> **SPEAKS LOUDLY ABOUT**
> ———————
> **WHO WE ARE AS CHRISTIAN PEOPLE."**
> ———————
> —Thom Schultz, *Group*, September 1986, p. 10

Everyone agrees that youth should "be" and "do" together so that they experience the church as a warm and safe place to be. But everyone does not agree on how to foot the bill.

Most youth groups have used fund-raising to foot the bill for their youth ministry programs. But fund-raisers wear out youth groups, their parents, and their churches. Often parents say they would rather just give the money than bake another pie. Fortunately, fund-raising is not the only way to foot the bill for youth ministry.

CHALLENGE THE YOUTH TO PAY

Strategy 1: As part of their discipling experience in the youth group, every Christian young person should be learning the importance of giving a portion of income back to the Lord through the church. Though youth have the most discretionary income of any age-group, they are the least tapped financial resource for ministry in the church. In teaching stewardship to youth, an obvious place to begin is by inviting them to foot the bill for youth ministries from which they personally benefit.

- Step 1: Plan a youth group meeting where the budget—the actual cost of youth ministry—is presented to them, identifying monthly expenses.
- Step 2: Invite youth to anonymously write their monthly incomes on pieces of paper, then return their papers to a youth sponsor who totals the amounts.
- Step 3: Compare the total income with the expenses.
- Step 4: Discuss what percentage the youth are willing to give from their income to cover what percentage of the total cost of youth ministry.

The youth likely cannot or will not foot the whole bill. But setting small goals that can potentially increase is a good first step.

Strategy 2: Often an entire youth group can take advantage of short-term (one- to three-day) work opportunities to earn income for their youth ministry programs. Seasonal work is often suited to this strategy, though it may require some creative thinking and exploring. Sometimes a proposal made to a potential employer, with an explanation of the purpose, will lead to more income than most fund-raisers.

CHALLENGE THE CHURCH TO PAY

Strategy 3: Ask the church to consider adding youth ministry to the annual budget. Most churches foot the bill for their other ministry programs, but youth ministry is often an exception. Write up a clear proposal to the congregation, (1) describing the request, (2) itemizing and justifying the expenses, and (3) suggesting the advantages and benefits.

This is often all it takes to both get youth ministry on the budget and renew excitement for the youth ministry program in the congregation. It is exciting to imagine the time and energy youth

could invest in mission and outreach if they were no longer sad-
dled with the burden of fund-raising. Or, fund-raising can become
a ministry itself if the youth group does it on behalf of others.

Strategy 4: Fund-raising is still a common way youth
groups generate some of the income they need for youth ministry. Keeping a number of principles in mind will help it to be
more accepted in the congregation:

- Always report to the congregation how money will be
  used. After the activity, report to the congregation about
  the activity so they can share in the experience they
  helped fund.
- The youth group should always do the work necessary for
  a fund-raiser. Youth can buy the ingredients, bake the
  pies, and make the ice cream on Saturday before the ice
  cream social Sunday evening.
- Seriously consider giving a tithe of fund-raising efforts to
  some other ministry of the church, conference, or community.

CHALLENGE SOMEONE ELSE TO PAY

Strategy 5: An often overlooked source of income are grants
offered by individuals, corporations, or church agencies. Many of
these groups are interested in seeing youth develop leadership
and ministry skills. To encourage this, they create grants to help
send youth to leadership training events, seminars, and conferences. Grants may also be available to help start programs for
camping, day care, and outreach to the hungry or homeless.

The first step, of course, is to discover whether or not such
grants are available. When they are, they usually require an
application and a proposal. Conferences and social service
agencies can be helpful in uncovering potential grant sources
and in proposal writing. When grant money is received, it
should be used precisely as outline in the proposal.

These five strategies, taken together, can take some of the
financial frustration out of youth ministry. The key is finding creative ways to foot the bill for youth ministry.

CHAPTER 30
CONNECT WITH THE CONGREGATION

Orv and Paula had a tremendous youth ministry program. Youth regularly attended Wednesday night Bible studies, Sunday evening socials, and other youth group gatherings. In recent months, youth from the community were showing up at the invitation of youth group members. Parents were pleased, but congregational leaders were not.

Youth were not seen in Sunday morning worship. Youth were not seen at special evening worship and mission services. Youth were not seen in congregational meetings or service programs. Eventually, congregational leaders began to accuse Orv and Paula of running a separate youth church and wondered if it wasn't time for a change of leadership.

The youth group is, by its very nature, often separated from the life of the congregation. Youth are rightly identified as a group that has special ministry needs. Life for youth who want to follow Jesus Christ has never been more difficult. Therefore, giving special attention to their life experiences, issues, and decisions in an effort to "win" them for Christ and the church is entirely appropriate.

At the same time, this special ministry must be intentionally conducted in a congregational context. Youth, although they are a community of the Spirit as a youth group, are also a part of the larger community of the Spirit—their congregation, their denominational conference, and the church universal.

One aspect of discipling youth is to strengthen their ties to the church. Strong connections between the youth group and the congregation help prevent the problem Orv and Paula were beginning to face.

Congregations, however, must also decide that they want

youth involved in the life of the congregation. Youth, if they are to embrace the church, cannot just be seen and not heard. A good first step toward strengthening ties between youth and the church is for the youth leadership team and congregational leadership to meet to discuss and decide how youth can contribute to congregational life.

Divide a marker board down the middle. On the right, identify the places where youth could be involved: committees, worship, service, teaching, hospitality, maintenance, care of the elderly, Bible school, and any other settings in church life. Then, in the other column, brainstorm specific ways youth could serve in each congregational setting. Write down every idea suggested.

After generating a list, the youth ministry leadership team and the congregational leadership can discuss and edit the list. Before deciding to eliminate an option, it should be considered seriously and good reasons should be given with which everyone agrees. Serving the church is not a

> **"WHEN** YOUTH EXPERIENCE LIFE IN THE CHURCH, THEY ARE MORE LIKELY TO REMAIN IN THE CHURCH."**
>
> —Robert Gribbon, *Developing Faith in Young Adults*, p. 68

place for prejudice because of age, lack of experience, or misconceptions about what youth can do.

Choose three new areas of involvement for youth to connect with the congregation. Print invitations to youth to consider their gifts and commit to one of the three options for plugging into congregational life. Expect and assume their involvement, rather than asking if they are interested. Youth sometimes pick up clues that they may not really be wanted or misinterpret words because they expect not to be really wanted. When a church has no tradition of youth involvement in congregational life, the language of the invitation is important.

Once youth begin to express interest in participating in church life, get commitments from them and hold them accountable, just as any church member would be. At the same time, adults need to be prepared to walk with youth as they learn what is required to do the task and to meet congregational expectations. Early success is crucial for youth and the congregation and leadership.

Youth sponsors can give youth opportunities to report on their work in the congregation. If they are serving on a committee, they can report on the committee's work. If they are teaching, they can share the joys and challenges, or they can share what they themselves are learning through the teaching process. If they are working in maintenance, they can share the struggles and needs of maintaining a place for worship and congregational life. Whatever their responsibilities, youth are affirmed when others take an interest, and, by sharing, they model involvement to others in the youth group who are either reluctant or waiting their turn.

The youth group is the training ground for responsible life in the faith community, but at some point, youth must begin exercising their gifts and talents in that faith community. It will be easier when their peers and their youth sponsors walk with them in those first steps of congregational involvement.

TEN WAYS YOUTH CAN CONTRIBUTE TO THE LIFE OF THE CONGREGATION

1. Create a banner for a special worship or sermon series.
2. Give the custodian a vacation and clean the church.
3. Give the ushers a break and take the offering, or become an usher team for a while.
4. Provide coffee, hot chocolate, and juice at a church gathering like the annual business meeting.
5. Teach or be a teaching assistant for a Sunday school or Bible school class.
6. Sing in the choir or play piano.
7. Bring flowers or other decorations for the morning worship service or a holiday season.
8. Be the welcoming committee for a month.
9. Create a periodic newsletter that describes what's going on in the lives of youth and in the youth ministry program.
10. Claim a bulletin board to report about youth activities.

YOUTH GROUP
CONGREGATIONAL INVOLVEMENT WORKSHEET

Congregational Settings	Specific Tasks

Three opportunities for new youth involvement in the life of our congregation:

1. _____

2. _____

3. _____

CHAPTER 31
SUPPORT GRADUATES

Mac's head danced with dreams and visions of college life; then he got there. His roommate smoked; he didn't. His floor partied; he didn't. Everybody had friends; he didn't know a soul. College life didn't match his dream. Nor did college studies. His classes were huge, his homework overwhelming, and the professors didn't even want to know his name. He was a freshmen, a number, alone. Mac wondered if he would survive the first semester.

For some youth the thought of college conjures up excitement; for others, dread. Few of either group have any idea what it will really be like, but they do have dreams—dreams of independence, of fun, of getting on

"SPIRITUAL DEVELOPMENT DOES NOT END AT GRADUATION."

with adult life. Even though college can be one of the most exhilarating times of life, it rarely lives up to the dreams.

College is a time of transition into the adult world. College encourages independence as young people learn to live on their own, take care of their own health, and provide for their own needs. College requires self-motivation. Students must develop their study skills, manage their time, and determine their priorities. College also presents challenges. Students confront different beliefs, ideas, and lifestyles. Adjusting to all these new experiences can be difficult.

The work world is also a leap into reality for most youth. They suddenly discover that someone else demands and even controls their time. They must learn to do their jobs well all day long. The cost of taxes, gas, and insurance can come as a shock for youth who have never before had to pay for job expenses.

Whether youth go to college or go to work, graduation is not a good reason to end a relationship with the youth group and the church, at least in the first year or two. Especially at this time, youth need to know they have friends and a community that remembers them, prays for them, and welcomes them home. When youth graduate from high school, the youth group can still serve its absent members.

Prepare. The youth group can prepare youth for graduation and the break from home, church, and community. Every year, the youth group should spend some time addressing this life transition. Engage youth in studies and conversations about work and whether or not to go to college or pursue training in some other setting. With those considering further schooling, discuss how to choose a school and a course of study. With those beginning a career, explore how to make good career choices and how to decide where to work. The youth group may also enjoy visiting prospective schools or employers as an outing. Finally, some youth may need help in applying for jobs or colleges, preparing for interviews, and managing money.

Send. Capitalize on youth's love of parties by having a send-off party for youth going away to work or school. These "blessing parties" can include gifts for the single life ahead, humorous prophecies about future goals and accomplishments, and remembrances of life in the youth group. After the "blessing party," celebrate the moment of departure or the first day of work by meeting at the person's home and driving with him or her out of town or to the new job. Once the custom gets started, it will trigger many creative ideas for blessing graduates.

Connect. Every youth who goes to college or goes to work struggles through an initial adjustment with occasional periods of homesickness and loneliness. When the youth group intentionally keeps connected to graduates, these times are easier to survive. Here are ten quick ideas for ministry to graduates:

1. Pray together for the graduates.

2. Create a graduate bulletin board with pictures, new addresses, birthdays, and favorite cookies or candy.

3. Send birthday cards, or send cards for no particular reason.

4. Send a youth group care package.

5. Invite graduates to share stories or make presentations to the youth group.

6. Send graduates the youth group newsletter or the church bulletins, after the youth group has annotated them.

7. Provide a subscription to the denominational magazine.

8. Get some of the youth group together and drop in for a visit at work or school. Prior permission from employers or administration is a good policy.

9. Provide child care for parents so they can visit the graduate.

10. Send a videotaped report or greeting.

Welcome. Many youth groups have discovered that welcoming graduates back into the youth group for special activities or at holidays during the first year after graduation is a positive experience for both the graduate and the youth group. Graduates usually bring back a maturity that high school youth quickly notice and admire. Graduates can also tell stories that will help prepare the next group of graduates. Although some graduates may not let go of the youth group when they should, this is less likely if graduates receive intentional invitations to specific activities, and youth sponsors distinguish between the graduates and the youth still in the youth group. Most graduates quickly move beyond the interests and behaviors of their high school years and graciously disconnect from the youth group.

The community life of a youth group can be a powerful experience, too powerful to abruptly end at transitions. Connections to this community can ease many of the changes that graduates face. It is simply a matter of preparing, celebrating, staying connected, and welcoming graduates back to their home.

PART 4
MIS-SION

C H A P T E R   3 2
ENCOUNTER CROSS-CULTURAL MISSION

Paul loved Spanish, and he knew that the best way to learn Spanish was to go where it is spoken. During the summer after his junior year, Paul's chance came and he spent three weeks in Guatemala. He came home enthused. He had encountered a different world. He had learned the power of humility and sharing. He had realized his privilege and some of the responsibility it brings. And he had discovered how to share his own faith more freely. Three weeks of encountering mission changed Paul's life forever.

By just changing the name, Paul's story could be retold many times by many youth. Discovering cross-cultural mission, by its very nature, can change a young person's life. It invites youth to claim their faith. It invites youth to see God at work in other people's lives. It invites youth to participate in God's work in the world. It empowers youth to bring hope and light to others. It gives youth an opportunity to change the world. But, before cross-cultural mission can do any of these things, it must be experienced.

For many youth in the church, "mission" has become a cliché, a tired old word with little meaning. When youth hear the word, it may bring to mind images of boring missionaries, exotic dress, and African jungles. Confronting those images will probably be the first task of helping youth to discover mission.

Cross-cultural mission happens in many places and in many ways. It takes place in North America and the rest of the world.

It includes planting churches and building houses. It is done by seminary graduates and high school graduates from every country of the world. Mission is being redefined by God's Spirit and God's people. It has outgrown its old images.

"WHEN YOUTH DECIDE TO ACT, THINGS HAPPEN."

—David Howard, as quoted by Paul Borthwick in *Youth and Missions*, p. 34

The road to discovering cross-cultural mission begins with thirdhand encounters such as reading and hearing about mission. Further along, secondhand encounters invite indirect involvement through personal contact with people in cross-cultural mission settings. Firsthand encounters immerse youth in direct experiences of mission, usually for short terms.

THIRDHAND CROSS-CULTURAL MISSION ENCOUNTERS

1. Subscribe to a mission newsletter. The first place to check for youth resources about mission is with denominational offices and mission agencies. These organizations often publish newsletters that put mission in a very readable and interesting format. These newsletters usually include reports, correspondence, lists of needs, and invitations for help.

2. Study a mission curriculum.

3. Read about cross-cultural mission. Many novels and films either tell mission stories or address mission issues. Youth can be encouraged to do this reading either for pleasure or for school assignments.

4. Invite people who communicate well with youth to share about their mission experiences. Telling stories is far more effective than seemingly endless slide presentations.

5. Take the youth group to a conference, seminar, or workshop on mission.

SECONDHAND CROSS-CULTURAL MISSION ENCOUNTERS

6. Begin a correspondence with someone who is in a mission setting. Youth in mission settings with their parents, young

adults, and mission agency staff are often interested in both receiving and sending mail, especially if part of the intention is to help youth discover mission.

7. Involve the youth group in an intentional friendship with a youth group in a mission setting. Mission agencies can help arrange such relationships. If it is a North American setting, visits can be arranged for a firsthand encounter.

8. Adopt a mission family for a year. To develop a relationship with a family in a mission setting, the youth group can send correspondence, gifts, photographs, and videos, and pray regularly. This also supports and encourages the mission family.

9. Include missions in the youth group budget. Secondhand mission encounters can provide the necessary connection to help youth support missions financially. The youth group could target an amount each month or for the year as a goal for giving to an agency, a family, or a specific project.

10. Involve the youth group in a study of a particular mission setting that includes exposure to the culture, language, and history of the setting. By bringing in objects, foods, clothing, music, and other simulated experiences, youth encounter the mission setting as much as possible, short of an actual visit.

FIRSTHAND CROSS-CULTURAL MISSION ENCOUNTERS

Firsthand cross-cultural mission encounters are actual visits to mission settings. Although it is most realistic to visit North American mission settings, visits to Mexico and Central American mission settings can be affordable. Any visit requires good planning. The first and most important step, wherever a youth group may wish to go, is to find a host in the desired mission setting who will give your youth group the invitation and set everything up for the visit. Some mission settings are more suitable and more prepared for a visit than others. When the visit is welcomed, the necessary arrangements—travel, visas, health preparations, and the activities of the trip itself—can often be easily made with either the host setting or a cooperating mission agency.

Youth are an incredible force. They have energy and creativity that the church rarely taps. Yet, God continually called young people—Samuel, David, Jeremiah, Mary, and Timothy—into missionary service of all forms. God still calls young people. Firsthand, secondhand, and thirdhand mission encounters can help them see that cross-cultural missions is essential to Christian faith and to their growing faith. When this happens, youth will discover God's "missionary" call upon their lives. The youth group, youth sponsors, and the church can help steer youth down that road so God's call can be heard.

C H A P T E R 3 3
DISCOVER THE WORLD

Jared came from a small town. His world consisted of games, girls, and grades, usually in that order. Although his faith was deep, his world was very small until a cold Saturday night when Jared's youth group went to hear Jesse Jackson speak. When that night was over, Jared realized the world was bigger than his school, church, and community. It included other Christians who held their faith deeply, even though they claimed a different denomination, ethnic heritage, and personal history. Jared realized there was a world that he too should care about.

One task of adolescence is to develop personal identity. Youth ministry, therefore, tends to concentrate on self-esteem issues and identity-building activities. Yet, most youth are also beginning to discover the world around them. Interest in the opposite sex, exploring career options, and experimenting with "worldly" lifestyles are examples of this growing awareness. There are three reasons the church and its youth should learn about the world and learn to love the world:

> **"LET** ALL THE CHRISTIANS OF THE WORLD AGREE THAT THEY WILL NOT KILL EACH OTHER."
>
> —John K. Stoner, Mennonite Central Committee poster

First, God loves the world. Many Christians are so influenced by the individualism of North American society that they focus only on the personal side of Christian faith. This focus on self is what makes it possible for some Christians to justify prejudice, indifference, hate, greed, and violence. Youth, as they explore Christian faith, are vulnerable to this influence. But, those who would love God must learn to love the world as God loves it.

Second, the church is in the world. The worldwide church is unknown to most Christians in North America. Yet, around the world, brothers and sisters in Christ share many of the same struggles and hopes. At the same time, many face problems and struggles that North Americans can barely imagine. Youth need to realize that they have an important relationship to their Christian peers in other countries, one that transcends community and national boundaries.

Third, the church's mission is to the world. Every Christian, young and old, is called to bring the gospel of Jesus Christ to the world. Youth need to discover this world to which they have been called, whether it is in their own backyard or on the other side of the globe. They must experience the same compassion for the world that led Christ to the cross.

The only way anyone can learn to love something is to spend time with it, learn to know it, discover its needs, and share its joys. But discovering and loving the world is not the end; it is the means to the end of bringing God's love into the world just as Jesus did. Knowing the world invites understanding, compassion, and involvement.

TEN WAYS TO INVITE YOUTH TO DISCOVER AND LOVE THE WORLD:

1. Encourage youth to learn a language, especially one—like Spanish—that provides opportunities for real conversations with people youth will encounter.

2. Occasionally host an international meal for the youth group. Many people who have lived in other cultures have learned to prepare distinctive foods. They are usually excited to open the eyes and palates of youth.

3. Focus on a country. Decorate the youth room with posters, colors, and artifacts from other places. Invite guests who have lived in or visited the country. Study its history. Learn the story of the church in that country.

4. Listen to world music. Often the only world music that youth have heard is either classical music or rock and roll. But

youth tend to be very open-minded about music. Usually, all they need is the opportunity to hear.

5. Sponsor an international student. One of the best ways to create world awareness is to invite someone from another country or cultural background into the youth group experience. Encouraging a family to host an international student not only provides a wonderful opportunity to that student but also benefits the youth group and the church family.

6. Sponsor a cross-cultural trip. Although this can be a challenging and expensive enterprise, it can have incredible rewards well worth the cost. It is also important to remember that cross-cultural experiences can happen within North America. Some denominations have programs that provide these opportunities for high school youth.

7. Encourage youth to read novels by international authors or about international settings. Or view an appropriate international film as a youth group activity. Or subscribe to an international magazine.

8. Study another religion. Use a curriculum and include guests who have had firsthand encounters with the religion being studied.

9. Begin a correspondence with someone living in a different culture.

10. Take the youth group to a lecture or a celebration that will help broaden their world experience. Many cities and communities have annual ethnic celebrations, including Black History month, Native Powwows, the Chinese New Year celebration, and Hispanic festivals.

When the youth group helps youth discover the world, they meet people, hear stories, share struggles, and become compassionate. This compassion can then be translated into a love that motivates youth to enter that world in the name of Jesus Christ. This entry into the world can invite radical changes in behavior, lifestyle, beliefs, and vocation—changes that help youth move from a heart faith to a lived faith. It is a love for the world that can invite youth to give their entire life to Christ and the work of the kingdom.

CHAPTER 34
SHARE FAITH

Gary was walking along the highway sobbing as Jim drove by. When Jim noticed him, he quickly drove the last few blocks to church, rushed out of the car, and ran to meet Gary to find out what was wrong. Gary told Jim that he had just been at the mall talking with people about his faith, but no one wanted to listen. Some had even made fun of him. Although Jim wasn't surprised at their response, he was amazed at the despair Gary felt for those who did not want to hear God's good news, especially complete strangers. Jim could never imagine having the courage to share his faith, even with friends.

Most youth can identify with Jim long before they can identify with Gary. Yet many share Gary's concern for others and his desire to share his faith. Many churches and youth groups also place a great deal of emphasis on being able to articulate and share the Christian faith. But with few skills, little training, and even less tact, too many youth find themselves walking a tightrope made slippery by the fears and guilt of messed-up, missed, and ignored opportunities to share their faith.

> **"REAL**
>
> **EVANGELISM IS ABOUT**
>
> **SHARING CHRISTIAN LOVE."**
>
> —Steve Clapp, *Peer Evangelism*, p. 4

Many youth struggle with sharing their faith. In spite of a faith in Christ that is strong and deep; in spite of being highly motivated to share their faith with others; in spite of the fact that they may often be challenged to do evangelism; most youth are rarely equipped for the task. When the opportunity does arise, many discover how ill-prepared they are. Unable to remember Scripture passages, defenseless against tough questions, and struggling to clearly present their own testimony, too many youth either avoid the subject of their faith altogether or they are plagued by fear and guilt. This is sad when their desire to share and their concern for the spiritual life of others is so real.

The answer, of course, is to help youth learn skills for sharing their faith. Before youth can share their faith, however, they must own it for themselves. Parents, youth sponsors, and pastors must challenge youth who are regular participants in the youth group to claim and profess faith in Jesus Christ. But once youth own their faith, if they are given the necessary tools, they can and will share their faith.

SIX STEPS TO SHARING FAITH:

1. Pray. Through prayer we can invite the Holy Spirit to touch the heart of a person who is hearing the good news. The youth group can become a place for prayer as its members go forth bearing good news among their friends. Pray for those with whom faith is shared. Pray for the person who is sharing. And pray for the words or actions that will be shared.

2. Learn to articulate faith. The youth group can provide opportunities for youth to learn how to talk about their faith. Youth can be encouraged to write down their faith stories or their views on faith issues. They can practice writing or speaking to different ages and groups. How would faith be shared with a fourteen-year-old, a twenty-eight-year-old, a Muslim friend, a sister? How can specific questions be answered? What responses are there to other religions? Role playing can be an effective way to practice talking about faith.

3. Build relationships. Faith is best shared with friends. Youth can be encouraged to develop relationships with others who are not Christian, not just to set someone up for evangelism, but as an expression of Christian love. Virtually everyone struggles with faith questions. Friendships provide opportunity and trust to struggle openly and honestly with faith questions.

4. Learn how to ask questions. Open-ended, invitational questions allow people the opportunity to express their views and their struggles. Youth can learn and practice creating faith questions without yes or no answers. For example: How do you know if something is right or wrong? Where is God when a tragedy happens? What do you expect the future will hold? These questions invite a conversation that can provide opportunity for the fifth step.

5. Share personal experiences of faith. Youth can tell how God, through Jesus Christ, has touched their own lives. This is a far more powerful witness than quoting doctrines and clichés. When the opportunity arises, youth can tell their own stories or the stories of people they know. They can share their struggles and their triumphs. They can share their peace and hope.

6. Pray again. People come to faith through the work of the Holy Spirit. We can tell the story; after that God is responsible. But prayer for the person and the message should continue.

Sharing faith with a friend is the greatest gift anyone can ever give a friend. It is also one of the most rewarding acts of the Christian life. Youth groups that discover the power and joy of sharing faith not only spread the good news but also build the church. It is the best way to make a small youth group bigger—mission in your own backyard!

HOW TO INVITE OPPORTUNITIES FOR SHARING FAITH:

1. Be an example. A lived faith is far more powerful than a professed faith.

2. Invite a friend to a youth group activity.

3. Critique media abuses of language, violence, sex, alcohol, drugs, and people.

4. Carry and read a Christian book on a tough issue, then discuss it with friends.

5. Take a countercultural, yet kingdom position, on war, materialism, or racism.

6. Perform random acts of kindness.

7. Participate in a voluntary service experience.

8. Listen to Christian rock music.

9. Celebrate Easter and Christmas as real Christian holidays and ignore the cultural celebrations.

10. Tell the story of Jesus Christ to someone.

CHAPTER 35
PROCLAIM JUSTICE

For Kim and Eric it was a break from school—a January trip to repair homes after a tornado. They had never hung drywall or mudded joints, but they were quick learners. The woman they were working for had been ripped off by a contractor. When she paid him, he skipped town, leaving the job unfinished. Sensing the injustice, Kim, Eric, and the others they were with worked hard. As the service project neared its end, Kim and Eric learned that the woman's nephew had also been ripped off by the same contractor. They decided to act. Skipping all other activities, Kim and Eric drywalled and mudded a three-bedroom house in two days. It was the beginning of putting things right.

Youth know the meaning of justice. From fair grading to proper calls on the basketball court, youth understand that people should be treated in right ways, with fairness. But they, like all of us, struggle to apply justice consistently. Often youth will cry injustice when they are its victims, but seem blind to it when they are its perpetrators. Some of the biggest ethical problems in the lives of youth today are justice issues. Recent research indicates that too many youth regularly cheat in school, too many guys take advantage of girls in relationships, and too many youth tell lies and steal.

Youth are also quite selective in responding to injustice that hurts others. Kim and Eric's example is not unusual. When youth see injustice happening to people outside their circles, their passions are aroused and, if they can, they act. But when

> **"YOUTH**
> **CAN MAKE**
> **A DIFFERENCE."**
>
> —Tony Campolo, *Ideas for Social Action*, p. 9

youth see injustice happening to those they know—a sister or brother, the "geeky" kid in their class, or a teacher—they rarely protest. In fact, youth will sometimes go to extremes to rationalize unjust behavior, commenting that those who were hurt deserved it or brought it upon themselves.

CONFRONT INJUSTICE

Yet, most youth know that injustice is wrong. The youth group can be a setting where youth reflect on justice issues and think about how they can make a difference. One way to increase awareness of injustice is to put three sheets of paper in the youth room, one titled "My experiences of injustice," the second titled "My acts of injustice," and a third titled "My observations of injustice." Over a period of several weeks, invite youth to write on these "graffiti walls."

A second way to increase youth's awareness of injustice and questions of justice is with field trips and group activities.

1. Enter an urban encounter experience.
2. Visit an Indian reservation.
3. Read the newspaper or watch the news together.
4. Visit city, state, or federal legislative meetings.
5. Interview employees of large corporations.
6. Talk with representatives of minority groups.
7. Observe court proceedings.
8. Walk the mall.
9. View an appropriate movie or watch TV together.
10. Observe school life.

REFLECT ON INJUSTICE

When the passions of youth have been aroused by exposure to injustice, they often feel the need to learn about justice and injustice and reflect on it.

1. Bible study is the necessary starting point because God's act of making things right with humanity and creation through Jesus Christ is the defining foundation for justice. Many stories in the Bible speak to justice issues.
2. Alongside Bible study should be study of the issue in con-

temporary society. News magazines can be a helpful resource.

3. Use a curriculum that addresses justice/injustice issues, or participate in mediation training.

4. Invite youth to reflect on the issues through journaling or writing poems and songs.

5. Many rock songs, both old and new, are thoughtful explorations of justice issues and help youth enter into learning and reflection.

6. Some films also offer helpful perspectives. Youth can be encouraged to observe, discover, and record how a film speaks about justice/injustice.

7. Guests can present their experiences of justice/injustice and what they learned from those experiences.

8. Youth can be encouraged in small groups to come up with proposals for addressing justice issues and righting the wrongs of injustice.

9. The books, speeches, and recordings of well-known justice advocates can be studied.

10. Explore the hymnal and other worship resources to discover how the church has addressed justice/injustice issues through its worship.

ACT ON BEHALF OF JUSTICE

Christian faith is a faith that acts. Exposure, learning, and reflection invite response, but it's easy to feel overwhelmed by the immensity of injustice and fail to do anything. The youth group, as a community of faith, can offer youth the opportunity to work together for justice so that none will feel overwhelmed or alone. It can also function as an accountability group that not only holds youth to their commitment to justice but also keeps justice in perspective as an act of discipleship that grows out of a commitment to follow Jesus Christ. Finally, the youth group provides a setting for youth to experience support, encouragement, and reflection on their justice work.

Acts of justice need not be big public events. Youth groups can engage in justice activities and proclaim justice in ways that make profound changes in their own lives or the lives of others.

RESPONSES TO "MY EXPERIENCE OF INJUSTICE":

1. Make a group commitment to "planned" random acts of kindness in response to unjust situations.

2. Role-play, practice, and then implement nonviolent rescue interventions on behalf of each other in response to specific injustices listed.

3. Help youth learn how to expose, confront, and stand against perpetrators of injustice.

RESPONSES TO "MY ACTS OF INJUSTICE":

4. Invite youth to confess personal acts of injustice within the youth group and seek counsel to learn better responses.

5. Invite youth to brainstorm possibilities, then make commitments to alter the lifestyle choices that involve them in injustice. These may include how they spend money, what they see and listen to, and the language they use.

6. Prepare prayers, meditations, and other worship elements for a youth-led worship service that confesses involvement in injustice and proclaims God's call to justice.

RESPONSES TO "MY OBSERVATIONS OF INJUSTICE":

7. Get involved with an agency that is working to prevent or respond to injustice.

8. Help the church and youth group to become a haven of safety for youth.

9. Encourage youth to take advantage of the opportunities they have to participate in the systems that can promote justice such as congregational leadership roles, school government, and peer advocacy and mediation programs.

10. Teach peers and younger children about justice and injustice.

Injustice is a pervasive force that can only be overcome by a deep belief that the power of God will eventually reign. Youth can participate in that power as they commit themselves to proclaiming justice as one aspect of following Jesus Christ.

CHAPTER 36
SEEK PEACE

The youth group was being torn apart by school rivalry. Last night's game had only escalated the tensions. Although Kristin had been fighting the problem at every possible point, she knew tonight could be a crisis moment. When she arrived at church, she asked her sponsors if she could open with prayer. Her words were simple yet powerful: "Let not the things of this world overwhelm our relationships in the youth group. So be it." Everyone knew what Kristin meant. In a breath, the Holy Spirit through Kristin had created peace.

Peace is often thought of as an international concern, but for Christians, peace encompasses all of life. It is grounded in our reconciliation with God which arises out of the salvation we experience in Jesus Christ. This peace we seek is a peace not only with God but also with others and the world. It includes personal, family, community, national, and international relationships. It includes all of the world that God loves and with which God seeks reconciliation. No one is left out.

Jesus is the example for peace seekers and peacemakers. In five ways Jesus sought and made peace:

- **Jesus began with an attitude of love.** Jesus showed us who to love and how to love everyone unconditionally.
- **Second, Jesus lived a life of kindness.** Although occasionally angry, Jesus was always kind. Compassion and healing dominated Jesus' daily life.
- **Jesus responded to injustice with words and symbolic acts of resistance.** He never responded to people with vengeance and violence.
- **Jesus expressed forgiveness.** Jesus knew that the most profound act of peacemaking was to offer forgiveness, even though sometimes the offer would be refused.

- **Jesus acted in service to others.** A lack of peace usually results from lack of concern for others. Jesus lived to serve others, even to the giving of his life.

Everyday in a multitude of settings—friendships and families, at school and work, at church and in the community—youth, to some degree, get caught in conflict. Until they become hard-hearted, most children and youth hate conflict. Yet most youth do not have strong skills for resolving conflict—skills that are increasingly important in a diverse society and world.

Jesus' five ways of seeking peace can guide us as we seek peace. They will not always be successful, just as they were not always successful for Jesus, but they are always the way to be faithful.

> **"DO** NOT
> **I DESTROY MY ENEMY**
> **WHEN I MAKE THAT**
> **PERSON MY FRIEND."**
> —Abraham Lincoln

SEEKING PEACE THROUGH THE YOUTH GROUP

1. *The search for peace on a personal level.*
- Invite youth to cultivate friendships with youth of a different ethnic or cultural background.
- Brainstorm a list of specific ways individuals can practice random acts of kindness in their school.
- Involve your youth group in a conflict resolution training experience.
- Occasionally provide opportunities within youth group worship for expressions of confession and forgiveness.
- Hold a foot-washing service.

2. *The search for peace within the family.*
- For one month, invite youth to record how often they say "I love you" to family members.
- Help youth create a "Covenant of Kindness" with a family member for a specific period of time.
- Brainstorm the words of violence youth use within their family.
- Just as Zacchaeus restored what he had stolen from the

poor, invite youth to identify "acts of restoration" they can use with their family.

- The youth group can prepare a "peace meal" for their families at church, including worship on the theme and ending with the Lord's Supper.

3. *The search for peace in the community.*

- Place a red rose in strategic community settings, such as the church, the school, or city hall.
- Provide a transportation service for the elderly.
- Boycott violent video games.
- Create and invite youth to participate in "peace gangs."
- Clean and restore a vacant lot.

4. *The search for peace in the nation.*

- Educate youth about political issues and how faith speaks to those issues.
- Invite youth of different ethnic or cultural backgrounds to participate in the youth group.
- Encourage youth to document their conscientious objection to participation in war or become peer educators about alternatives to military solutions.
- Challenge youth to examine their attitudes about violent entertainment, see its inconsistency with Christian faith, and remove it from their lives.
- Travel to your nation's capital to meet with members of the legislature and talk about political issues that affect youth and the church.

5. *The search for peace in the world.*

- Identify a country for the youth group to fall in love with. Discover its history, learn its language, and meet its people.
- Support an international service organization with money or material aid.
- Write letters advocating nonviolent and nonmilitaristic solutions to international conflicts.
- Identify the ways youth participate in the causes of pover-

ty and oppression in other countries, and make a commitment to change.
• Go on an international learning visit or service trip.

Seeking peace is a way of life best learned at a young age. Youth are at an ideal age to learn to seek peace, act to make peace, and be signs of the present and future kingdom of God.

CHAPTER 37
CONFRONT CULTURE

After viewing a video about rock music, Mary and the others in the youth group had a lot to think about. Following Jesus was really important to Mary, but she had never thought about how her faith might affect her choice of music. She had always enjoyed hard rock, although she knew some of it promoted values she considered wrong. The video had made her think. Over the next couple of days, Mary looked at her CDs, examining the cover art and reading the lyrics. After praying about it, Mary came to a decision. She discarded many of those CDs whose messages were inconsistent with her Christian faith. For Mary, it was a conversion experience.

Mary's story shows what can happen when youth are challenged to critically confront the culture they so readily absorb. Intuitively, youth know that elements of their culture clash with their Christian faith. They engage in a constant struggle with the world as they work to clarify their beliefs, their commitments, and the direction of their lives. As a part of this struggle, they often question and challenge their beliefs or explore new beliefs. They may abandon teachings of the church that they are not able to embrace. They may commit themselves to causes, behaviors, and institutions that take them away from following Jesus Christ. When youth are not encouraged to question their culture, examine their values, and commit to Christian discipleship, they are easy prey for a culture that wishes to consume them.

Youth, as well as adults, need to be challenged to critique their culture out of a Christian worldview. Too few youth realize the ways they are influenced, manipulated, and even oppressed by cultural forces. Youth who would follow Jesus Christ need to confront every element of their lives—sports, school loyalties, jobs, the use of money, career plans, music, dress and fashion, sexual standards, movies and television, books and magazines, and political interests.

Confronting culture gives youth power to live life more meaningfully and follow Jesus Christ more faithfully. It encourages them to expose their compromises and honestly declare their allegiance. It opens their eyes to the ways they have bought into the oppression and victimization of themselves and others by culture. It allows youth to experience solidarity with Christian youth in other countries who are also being oppressed by their cultures. Finally, confronting culture teaches youth to discern between those elements of culture that promote life and those that destroy life.

> **"THE UNEXAMINED LIFE IS NOT WORTH LIVING."**

Every culture consists of some positive elements, some negative elements, and some that are morally neutral. Youth, therefore, need to develop a critical Christian conscience so they can celebrate the good, denounce the evil, and minister to the needs their culture is trying to satisfy. After identifying a cultural element, youth sponsors can help youth critique it by using the five elements of Bible study method: focus, connect, dig, reconnect, and respond.

1. **Focus** the issue—by inviting youth to see the issue in a new light or from a different perspective.

- Music. View a music video and discuss these questions: What does the religious imagery communicate? How are women treated? What answer is offered to the problem? What is the predominant value?

- Sports. Watch several football or basketball games. Discuss: Who is the real winner in organized sports? How much time and what level of allegiance is expected? Who owns the athletes?

- Junk food. Invite youth to abstain from an agreed list of junk food for one week and then share their losses and gains from the experience.

2. **Connect** with the issue—by inviting youth to express their personal experience.
- Language. Choose a language issue, such as swearing, rudeness, inclusivity, or racial/ethnic jokes. Create a chart on which youth can monitor their language for one week.
- Work. Invite youth to compare their present levels of work, study, play, and worship to the levels they hope to have in ten years.
- Sitcoms. Watch a sitcom and discuss how family, gender, religion, sex, or race is portrayed.

3. **Dig** into the issue—by inviting youth to study and learn about the issue.
- Politics. Compare party platforms and discuss how Christian values agree with or disagree with the different views.
- Alcohol. Invite youth to survey their peers in their high schools about alcohol use and the reasons it is used.
- Movies. View a movie and analyze how the characters are portrayed, what message is conveyed, and how real life is betrayed.

4. **Re-connect** personal experience with the issue—by inviting youth to share how new information has influenced their view.
- Pornography. Ask youth to write a private statement about pornography that reflects their personal views as a Christian.
- Fashion. Invite youth to give one-tenth of their wardrobe to an agency that distributes used clothing.
- The car. Ask youth to describe their driving habits to one another. Then have them discuss the reasons for their willingness or unwillingness to honestly describe those habits.

5. **Respond** to the issue—by inviting youth to take an action that reflects a new view of the issue.
- Money. Invite youth to make a commitment of a certain amount of their income to support a mission effort of their congregation.

- Sex. Encourage youth to make a commitment to abstinence and publicly share that commitment within the youth group so they can support and encourage one another.
- School. Empower youth to take the opportunities they have to address the school system by accompanying them to a school board meeting.

All of these examples help youth to confront the culture they live in and see how it impacts their lives and the lives of others. Sometimes its influences are positive, sometimes negative. By becoming more aware of the cultural pressures on them, Christian youth can develop a critical Christian conscience that enables them to reject cultural values that compromise their allegiance to Christ and to their brothers and sisters across cultures.

CHAPTER 38
PROVIDE SANCTUARY

Elton was the typical nerd. When he started high school he was 4'11" tall, weighed ninety pounds, had just gotten braces, and desperately wanted to play on the basketball team. He got cut the first day of tryouts. But in the youth group, Elton was appreciated for his sense of humor, his thoughtful contributions to Bible studies, and his emerging leadership skills. Through his four years of high school, Elton's deep faith shone in the church and among his friends. Although high school never was a comfortable place, the church always was. It was his sanctuary.

Many youth feel alienated—from their families, school, and society. They are the "computer nerds." They are the "intellectuals." They are the African-Americans, Hmong, Native Americans, and Hispanics. They are the "grungers." They are the "abstainers." Like Elton, they are pushed out to the fringes, into subcultures, because they either can't or choose not to fit into the mainstream mold. Typically they either find each other or get lost in the uncaring crowds. Occasionally they find sanctuary in the church—a place where they don't even have to fit into the subculture mold.

One of Jesus' great gifts was his ability to reach out to the marginalized people—tax collectors, women, publicly declared sinners, children. Jesus spoke to them, touched their lives, and welcomed them into his family of faith. In Jesus these people found acceptance, new life, and a family of faith that followed Jesus' example and welcomed them.

To be a sanctuary—a place where youth in the subcultures can be accepted and encouraged to new life—is one of the greatest gifts the church can offer. Within the church, youth groups can be the best bearers of this gift. But to be a sanctuary means going a step beyond being a welcoming youth group. It means deciding to reach out to a specific subculture of youth. It means assessing your youth group environment to identify changes that need to be made to effectively incorporate and minister to that subculture. Finally, ministry to a youth subculture will mean creating settings that minister to the specific needs of those youth. To be a sanctuary is to be in mission.

REACH OUT

The church in North America is mostly middle- to upper-middle-class, and white. Worshipers gather on Sunday morning and sing 100- to 400-year-old hymns. They dress up for church and promptly head home for Sunday dinner. They affirm the preacher's prophetic challenges and go on living like everyone else in the world around them.

> **"NO** YOUTH IS OUTSIDE THE LOVE OF CHRIST."

Youth groups typically reflect their congregations. For a youth group, then, to decide to reach out to a youth subculture is a big decision that may challenge church traditions and create discomfort. Minimizing this discomfort is crucial because subculture youth can find sanctuary in the church only when they find acceptance.

STEP 1: COUNT THE COST.

The youth group must understand that what they are about to do is mission. It will require prayer, learning, and developing cross-cultural sensitivity. For example, if Hmong families are a part of your community, learn their story as you seek to include them in your ministry.

STEP 2: INVOLVE CHURCH LEADERS.

Pastors in particular may want to orient worship in new ways that will speak to a new audience. For example, if you want to invite youth immersed in the heavy metal rock subculture, it will be important to incorporate some contemporary forms of music into worship.

STEP 3: CLARIFY YOUR MISSION.

As a youth group, prayerfully determine the youth sub-culture to which you will reach out. Someone in the youth group may already represent the subculture. A youth group member may already have friends in the group. It may be a group that is not readily identifiable as a group, such as youth whose parents are divorced or youth who have experienced abuse.

ASSESS

Every youth group has an inside language everyone under-stands, unwritten rules everyone knows, expectations everyone shares. Groups have assumptions about participation, leader-ship, and commitment that everyone lives by. New youth won't know these things. The youth group must assess these things and intentionally tear down any potential barriers to making new youth feel included.

STEP 4: ASSESS WORSHIP.

How do you speak about, learn about, and understand a relationship with God? Evaluate everything from Bible study materials to music to forms of prayer in terms of how it will come across to a new group of youth. For example, youth can be confused by the many ways God is addressed. Yet constant references to God as "Father" may be a problem for youth who have been abused by a father figure.

STEP 5: ASSESS COMMUNITY.

Welcoming a youth subculture into the youth group com-munity means asking whether current activities tend to include or exclude these youth. For example, activities that cost money, such as bowling, may exclude youth who have very little. Or group hugs can make new people very uncomfortable, even exclude them.

STEP 6: ASSESS MISSION.

How does your youth group relate to the world around you? While most youth are well aware of the world of their peers, youth tend to assume they know more than they do, then act on their assumptions. For example, if youth assume that premarital sexual activity is wrong, can they extend grace to the new youth who has been sexually active? Could a service trip to the inner city be painful for someone who previously lived there?

CREATE NEW SETTINGS

Ministry to youth subcultures calls for risk-taking and change. But experimenting with new ministry ideas can also unleash creativity. It can unexpectedly meet the needs of youth already in the youth group and breathe new life into the church.

STEP 7: DRAW UP A PLAN.

Prepare written proposals—including purpose, objectives, strategy, and budget—for new programs and activities so the youth group and church leadership are completely informed. This information can head off criticism. For example, if the youth group is attending a powwow, explain what powwows are, their purpose in the aboriginal community, and what the youth group is expected to learn.

STEP 8: COVER YOUR BASES.

Work to insure that new youth ministry settings and experiences are consistent with your congregation's understanding of Christian faith and life. If you are uncertain, invite the pastor's perspective. For example, supporting youth who have received abortions may challenge the sensibilities of some in the congregation.

STEP 9: REPORT.

Always report to the youth group and the congregation how new programs, activities, and ministries are going. Criticism most often arises when people sense a lack of accountability or feel a lack of ownership.

A sanctuary for youth is not so much a place to escape as it is a place where it is safe for youth to be themselves. The church is fulfilling a key aspect of its mission when it offers these youth a safe place in an otherwise unwelcoming world.

CHAPTER 39
SEEK THE CITY

Irma was from a small town in a mostly rural part of the Midwest. Life was predictable. As the youth group president, she faithfully prepared devotions and agendas for every youth meeting. New on the agenda was the youth group's decision to attend the denominational youth gathering in downtown Chicago. As they studied the schedule and anticipated the experience, Irma realized that nothing would be predictable. They would decide whether to sort clothes at the new thrift store or shop at the new downtown mall. They would decide whether to play with kids at the Urban Center or play with the Cubs at Wrigley Field. They would decide whether to serve meals at the homeless shelter or eat meals at the Chicago Pizza Factory. They would decide whether to come home with nice memories or changed lives.

Many suburban and rural youth know the city. They know where to go shopping. They know where to party. They know where to watch their favorite teams play. They know where to eat. They know what parts to fear. They know the city in the same way they know insurance and groceries. They know what is there that meets their needs, even if they don't know how it got there, where it came from, and who made it possible. This is the city most youth know. It is the city portrayed in the media—the good stereotyped in advertising and the bad flaunted in movies. Rarely do youth see the city as a place of need, a place of life, a place God loves.

This is ironic, though, because these youth appear to be

> **"SEEK THE PEACE OF THE CITY AND PRAY TO THE LORD ON ITS BEHALF."**
>
> —Jeremiah, Jeremiah 29:7

more urban than suburban or rural. This does not mean they are streetwise. Rather, they are attracted to the trappings of urban life. They listen to its music. They dress according to its fashion. They try to speak its language, carry its attitude, and live its lifestyle as if they created it. Even though most suburban and rural youth don't really know the city, many of them are attracted to it, maybe because they expect it will one day be their home.

With over half the world's population living in cities, the city is fast becoming the most important setting for mission. Youth, who are going to study, work, and live in the city, need to experience the city as more than just a shopping, sports, and media center. The church can help youth get past the "nice place to visit" mentality so that they can discover the city as a place where real people live and a place where God's Spirit is at work. Youth groups can seek the city in several ways.

Reveal youth stereotypes of the city. Every person learns stereotypes from family, media, and their community. Here are some ways to help youth get beyond these stereotypes:

1. Invite youth in the group to tell stories of their experiences with the city. Analyze those experiences. Was it an urban or suburban experience? What descriptive words were chosen to tell about the experience and what do those words reveal? Who was encountered and what could be learned from those persons? What causes contributed to the experience and how might others involved in the experience have felt about those causes?

2. Study the media's portrayal of the city by watching television, viewing films, listening to music, and reading news magazines and newspapers. While doing this, invite a guest who actually lives in the city to help in the critique.

Discover the real world of the city. This is difficult to do as a visitor, but it is more likely to happen when a visit to the city is made with this intention. If they visit with a goal of discovery, youth will see and hear in new ways.

3. When visiting the city, plan encounters with the needs of the city. Visiting with people at homeless shelters, food pantries, and shelters for abused women and children help youth to see

that people in the city are hurting. Youth can begin to understand that cities are places where some people are poor, have little power, and are victimized by political structures.

4. Then visit places where great things are happening. Visiting with people at urban development projects, political empowerment groups, and community education centers shows youth that cities can be positive places where God is at work, where the church is in ministry, and where individuals can make a difference.

Discern the social crises of the city. Cities are places where the social problems of society are magnified and laid bare. Racism, poverty, alcoholism, inequality, oppression, and a host of other social ills can be encountered in their rawest forms. Youth who want to participate in the mission of the church in the city need to be aware of these problems and begin to understand their causes and solutions.

5. Teach the youth group about the social ills of the day, discovering what the Bible has to say, what the church has to say, and what other people have to say. During this teaching, look at the historical cause of the problems and invite guests to tell their stories of how these problems have touched their lives.

6. Dig into the polluted political realities of social problems. People caught in these problems are usually victims of political powers that gain from their difficult circumstances. Youth can be encouraged to study political systems and meet with politically involved people who can address the coercive powers that perpetuate the dark side of urban life.

Seek the good of the city. When the Israelites lived in the city of Babylon, God called them to seek the good of the city. They were to bring joy, life, and God to the city. This same message can still be applied today.

7. Develop a sister youth group relationship with an urban congregation. Meet together regularly in both churches. Encourage youth to visit each other's homes and schools. Encounter the city together and learn from each other.

8. Enter into regular service experiences in the city in your own backyard. This is the place where youth can most authenti-

cally develop understanding and relationships, and be transformed by ministry in the city.

There is no place and there are no people God does not
love. Youth from the suburbs and rural areas can never learn
this if they never encounter the city and its people by studying,
listening, and walking with people in the city. For any youth
group, the Jerusalem that Jesus called his disciples to is the city
in their own backyard. This may be the most profound lesson
youth can learn when they seek the city.

C H A P T E R   4 0
SERVE THE WORLD

Melissa was one of seven in her youth group who piled into a van and headed for Denver, Colorado. She had never been there and had never done what she was about to do. While she pounded nails, Melissa worked alongside Patrice, whose family would be moving into the house when it was done. While sorting clothes, Melissa visited with Mrs. Fischer, a woman who lived on the street. While serving soup, Melissa ate with a table full of children whose bright eyes and contagious laughter touched her heart. In the act of serving others, Melissa met people who had shown her Jesus, and her faith grew deep through the act of love.

There may be no youth group activity that can more profoundly change the lives of youth than a service experience. In service, youth confront themselves, their values, and their commitments. In service, youth confront the world, its hypocrisies, and its tragedies. In service, youth are confronted by God, the depth of love, and the miracle of salvation. When youth groups go on service trips, they see God's acts of salvation in the lives of those they meet. This often turns out to be far more important than the number of nails driven, clothes sorted, or meals served. No one can experience that and not be changed. If youth ministry is about calling youth and discipling youth to faith in Jesus Christ, then regular service projects should be a part of the mission experience of every youth group.

In reality, service experiences benefit the youth group as much as if not more than those who are served. This is okay as long as everyone is up front about it and the real emphasis is on relationships. If people experience the real care and compassion of youth, if they are treated with respect and understanding, and if they are lifted up and encouraged, then the service they receive from others is appreciated. Youth who serve must serve with faith, hope, and love for the people they are serving.

FOUR REASONS FOR SERVICE:

1. Service is an act of discipleship. Christians are called to continue the healing ministry of Jesus through service to others.

2. Service provides youth groups with an intensive experience that can draw them closer to God, each other, and to the world God loves.

3. Service gives youth a chance to discover that they can make a difference because they have the opportunity to meet real needs.

4. Service enlightens youth to their own participation in systems and behaviors that bring pain and misery to others. It also helps them to see how they are affected by these same systems.

THE SERVICE TRIP

Service trips span several days or weeks. They offer youth three benefits. First, youth can take on projects that require more time to complete. Second, youth experience the demands of cooperation and living together. Third, longer trips include time for reflection on the experience and the invitation for spiritual growth as a result of the experience. Once the idea for a service trip has been planted, the process for planning begins.

> **"EVERYONE**
>
> **CAN BE GREAT BECAUSE**
>
> **EVERYONE CAN SERVE."**
>
> —Dr. Martin Luther King, Jr.

STEP 1: DEFINE GOALS.

Before making any decisions, brainstorm with the youth group about the goals and purposes of the trip. Evaluate whether or not each activity contributes to these purpose and goals. Make sure the purposes and goals support the vision for youth ministry.

STEP 2: MAKE A DECISION.

There are two ways to do a service trip. The first and easiest is to contact a service agency and plug into their service programs for youth groups. This insures that all the details are covered. The second way is to create your own service experience. The initial decision must include several options about where the youth group would like to go and what they would like to do. Then contact churches or agencies in those areas and inquire about the possibilities. A key to successful service experiences is to start small.

STEP 3: NEGOTIATE THE EXPERIENCE.

Once the where and what decisions are made, it is time to begin investigating and negotiating the details. Determine dates, service/mission assignments, room and board, and local costs.

STEP 4: ENLIST SUPPORT.

When most of the details are worked out, it is helpful to prepare a written proposal that includes all the essential information. This proposal can be placed before the youth, their parents, and the congregation for support. Youth can make a commitment to go. Parents can make a commitment to send their youth. And the congregation can make a commitment to support the experience with prayer, finances, and words of encouragement.

STEP 5: PREPARE FOR THE TRIP.

Preparation for a service trip includes:
- setting up a youth group covenant which outlines group living expectations;
- preparation studies on mission, sharing faith, justice issues, and information about the service setting;
- logistical preparations concerning travel, appropriate dress, tools, meals, insurance, and etiquette in the service setting.

STEP 6: PACK AND GO.

STEP 7: DEBRIEF.

Upon the youth group's return, it is important to reflect on the experience—what was learned, how lives were changed. It is also necessary to report back to parents and the congregation through a newsletter, a bulletin board, or a special worship service.

EVERYDAY SERVICE

Service should not be limited to just an occasional trip. Youth groups can include service as a regular part of youth group activities. Most importantly, routine service experiences help youth integrate service into everyday living. They can also help prolong the "high moment" of a service trip, help youth constantly critique the prevailing cultural values, and help youth build a "world awareness."

TEN IDEAS FOR EVERYDAY SERVICE:

1. Initiate a once-a-month "Service on Saturday" to the congregation and the community.

2. Maintain a regular schedule at the local food pantry or homeless shelter.

3. Provide volunteer child care during congregational business meetings or other congregational activities.

4. Set up a volunteer schedule in a local thrift store.

5. Run a food collection service in the church and deliver the food to a food pantry.

6. Create intentional friendships with people in a nursing home or home for the elderly.

7. Develop an after-school tutoring service.

8. Set up an informal mentoring program between youth and children in the congregation.

9. House-sit and do chores for other church members so they can go on a service trip.

10. Become a litter removal crew for several streets or a stretch of highway.

In this self-serving and individualistic world, service to others can meet real needs that are often ignored. Serving others may be one of the easiest ways for youth to live out their faith. It rarely demands specialized skills but always demands time and a concern for others. This is why service is often among the most spiritually challenging experiences a young person will ever have.

At the same time, service can be a spiritually challenging experience for the recipients as they come face-to-face with youth who express God's love and turn upside down the negative stereotypes of youth culture. For many people, youth groups involved in service may be one of the most important ways the gospel is communicated.

CHAPTER 41
SHAPE MISSIONARY PEOPLE

Joann had always had a keen sense of God's call upon her life. In school, she was constantly challenging her friends with the demands of discipleship. In church, she eagerly listened to the stories of missionaries and service workers. Wherever Joann went, she touched people's lives with kindness and gifts of service. When Joann graduated from high school, she faced all the big decisions her friends faced. Although her career plans were uncertain, her vocational direction had been set. Through school and beyond, her life would be centered around service and mission. She had become a missionary person.

Youth like Joann are more common than we realize. They shatter our generalizations about youth and force us to re-evaluate our assumptions. Not all youth are completely self-centered. Not all youth are hopeless about their future and the future of the world. Not all youth have rejected Christian faith, the church, and its mission in the world.

On the contrary, the majority of youth in the church meet the basic requirements for becoming missionary people. Although they struggle with what they believe and how to live what they believe, most church youth want a close personal relationship with God and openly acknowledge a commit-

> ## "WE
> ## HAVE A
> ## WORLD TO WIN."
>
> —Paul Borthwick, *Youth and Missions*, p. 29

ment to follow Jesus. Most youth also want to make a positive difference in the world and believe they can have a significant influence in other people's lives. The challenge facing the church and the youth group is to capitalize on these positive professions about faith and life, and help youth become missionary people.

Missionary people are first of all those who actively seek first the kingdom of God. Their relationships, values, and decisions are influenced by the priority of the lordship of Jesus Christ. Youth seeking first God's kingdom are youth who continually ask the question, "What would Jesus do?"

Secondly, missionary people are people in training for the work of God's kingdom. They realize that in addition to depending upon God's Spirit, they must discover their gifts and learn skills to participate in God's work. Youth in training for God's work are preparing for more than a job; they are preparing for their life's vocations.

Third, missionary people are people who believe God's kingdom makes a difference in the world. They also believe God invites them to participate in making that difference. They are optimistic about what God is doing and what God can do through them. Youth in the kingdom of God make a difference in the world because God calls them and gives them the power.

But youth cannot become missionary people alone. They need the guidance and leadership of adults as they cultivate their relationship with God. They need the encouragement of their community of faith. They need support as they risk life in the world. Youth who desire to be missionary people need their youth group to help them:
- seek first God's kingdom,
- discern and prepare for the missionary vocation, and
- act in ways that make a kingdom difference in the world.

HELP YOUTH SEEK FIRST GOD'S KINGDOM BY...

Challenging youth to define their allegiance. Youth must constantly be reminded to examine whom they serve. Sports, academics, jobs, government, money, fashion, and desires all compete for the allegiance of youth. Missionary youth will give their allegiance to God alone.

- Youth can be challenged to choose between voluntary service or military service, football camp or a missions conference.
- Youth can be challenged to chart their time to discover where their hearts lie.

Opening their eyes to see Jesus wherever they go. In a world that categorizes, pigeonholes, boxes, and excludes people, youth must learn to see Jesus in all places and with all people. Missionary youth will bring good news to the poor, proclaim liberty to the oppressed, and restore hope to the hurting.

- Youth might try to walk in Jesus' shoes for a day and see every person with Jesus' eyes.
- Or, youth might see every person they meet for a day as if that person were Jesus.

Cultivating their compassion. There is no place in God's kingdom for hate, slander, cruelty, and disregard. Missionary youth will learn to cry and laugh with others. They will learn to suffer and serve with others. They will learn to mourn and triumph with others.

- Youth can ask "questions between the lines" that help them discover the root causes of evil.
- Youth can confront their privilege and struggle with its oppression.

HELP YOUTH PREPARE
FOR THE MISSIONARY VOCATION BY...

Developing a vision for the coming of God's kingdom. Christian faith boldly proclaims that God is in control and that God's vision for the world will prevail. Missionary youth will share that vision, not as an excuse for passivity but as an urgent call to action.

- Youth can be taught to identify, name, and expose evil.
- Youth can be challenged to think what it means to live each day as if Jesus would return tomorrow.

Discerning their gifts, talents, and skills. God has given gifts, talents, and the ability to learn skills to every person. They exist for the sake of the kingdom. Missionary youth will discover how to use these gifts for the sake of others.

- The gifts, talents, and skills of youth can be identified by adults and friends who know them well.
- Opportunities can be provided for youth to practice and use their gifts, talents, and skills.

Examining their education and career plans. One of the most important questions everyone answers is what they will do with their life. Youth entertain this question long before it is answered. Missionary youth will be looking for education and careers that allow them to serve God and the church.

- Youth can be encouraged to attend church-related colleges.
- Youth can be reminded to seriously consider church-related careers.

HELP YOUTH MAKE A KINGDOM DIFFERENCE IN THE WORLD BY...

Setting kingdom heroes before them. Church history is full of people whose lives changed the course of history in big and little ways. Every Christian inherits this history and can share in its power. Missionary youth will admire these heroes and seek to emulate them.

- Introduce present-day kingdom heroes to youth.
- Describe with respect the work of people who have given their lives to make a kingdom difference.

Addressing their fears. The task of serving God and the church is daunting. It has never been easy and it never will be. There is a cost to this discipleship. Missionary youth will see past the cost to the rewards.

- Invite people who make a difference to speak honestly about their fears and the dangers and how they have lived with them.
- Teach youth the skills of patience, perseverance, and simplicity so that some of their fears lose power.

Placing youth into missionary settings. No one can make a kingdom difference if they never leave the comfort of the church community. Jesus walked the roads, visited the homes, and entered the institutions of oppression. Missionary youth will follow Jesus into the places where the good news needs to be shared.

- Beginning in small ways, challenge youth to risk entering new places and new relationships.
- Walk beside youth as when they choose to confront the forces that overwhelm their world or the world of their friends.

Creating missionary people is a lifelong pursuit. It doesn't happen overnight and it may not happen during the four years of high school, but adolescence is the time in which to start. People are more receptive, more passionate, and more dedicated during their youth. In this soil, we can plant the seeds that will one day yield a harvest of missionary people.

RESOURCES FOR A YOUTH LEADER'S FIRST TOOLBOX

HELP, I'M A YOUTH LEADER!

Jones, Stephen D. *Faith Shaping: Youth and the Experience of Faith.*
Rev. ed. Valley Forge, Pa.: Judson Press, 1987.

This book is still the finest introduction to how young people
come to faith and grow in discipleship.

Welty, Lavon. *Blueprint for Congregational Youth Ministry.* Newton,
Kan. and Scottdale, Pa.: Faith & Life Press and Mennonite
Publishing House, 1988.

A foundational resource that invites seeing ministry with the
youth group as one of several youth ministry settings in every
congregation.

PART 1: LEADERSHIP

Schultz, Thom and Joani. *Kids Taking Charge: Youth Led Youth
Ministry.* Loveland, Colo.: Group Books, 1991.

The most important aspect of leadership in youth ministry is empowering youth to lead. Thom and Joani Schultz offer the necessary tools for creating youth-led youth groups.

Smith, Tim. *8 Habits of an Effective Youth Worker*. Wheaton, Ill.: Victor Books/Scripture Press, 1995.

Tim Smith focuses on the adult working with youth, emphasizing that you must care for yourself if you desire to care for others.

PART 2: WORSHIP

McNabb, Bill and Steve Mabry. *Teaching the Bible Creatively*. Grand Rapids, Mich.: Youth Specialties/Zondervan, 1990.

Recognizing that the Bible must be at the core of our teaching, McNabb and Mabry offer thirteen principles and loads of ideas for making Bible study—with or without curriculum—a creative, life-changing experience.

Sparkman, G. Temp. *Writing Your Own Worship Materials*. Valley Forge, Pa.: Judson Press, 1980.

The longevity of this book has proven its value. In an era of pre-packaged programs, Sparkman challenges, encourages, and guides you to create your own worship resources.

PART 3: COMMUNITY

Rice, Wayne. *Up Close and Personal: How to Build Community in Your Youth Group*. Grand Rapids, Mich.: Youth Specialties/ Zondervan, 1989.

Billed as a "complete community building kit," this book provides a theology for building community, a curriculum, and 131 more ideas for inviting youth to lean on and care for each other.

Sturkie, Joan and Siang-Yang Tan. *Peer Counseling in Youth Groups.* Grand Rapids, Mich.: Youth Specialties/Zondervan, 1992.

Youth will turn to their friends with problems before they turn to anyone else. With this truth in mind, Sturkie and Tan offer youth the necessary skills for helping their friends.

PART 4: MISSION

Borthwick, Paul. *Youth and Missions.* Wheaton, Ill.: Victor Books/Scripture Press, 1988.

Borthwick focuses on broadening the world view of youth so that they can see needs, discover God at work, and experience the power of making a difference in the name of Christ.

Clapp, Steve. *Peer Evangelism: Youth and the Big Scare E Word.* Elgin, Ill.: Brethren Press, 1993.

Mission to the world must begin with mission in everyday life. Clapp's curriculum gives youth the tools to overcome their hesitation and reach out to their friends with God's good news.

ABOUT THE AUTHOR

Mike Bogard is in his sixth year as youth minister for the Western District of the General Conference Mennonite Church. In addition to resourcing and consulting with congregations, Mike and a youth leadership team guide and direct area-wide youth events and programs.

Previously, Mike served for seven years as youth minister for the Northern District of the General Conference Mennonite Church. During four of those years he was also a high school Bible instructor. He has also been a pastor and a camp director.

Mike writes a regular column for *YouthGuide*, the youth ministry newsletter published by Faith & Life Press, and has written Bible study curriculum.

Mike and Marlene, along with their sons, Ben and Josh, live on a small acreage west of Newton, Kansas, with Sam the dog, Alice the goat, and several cats.